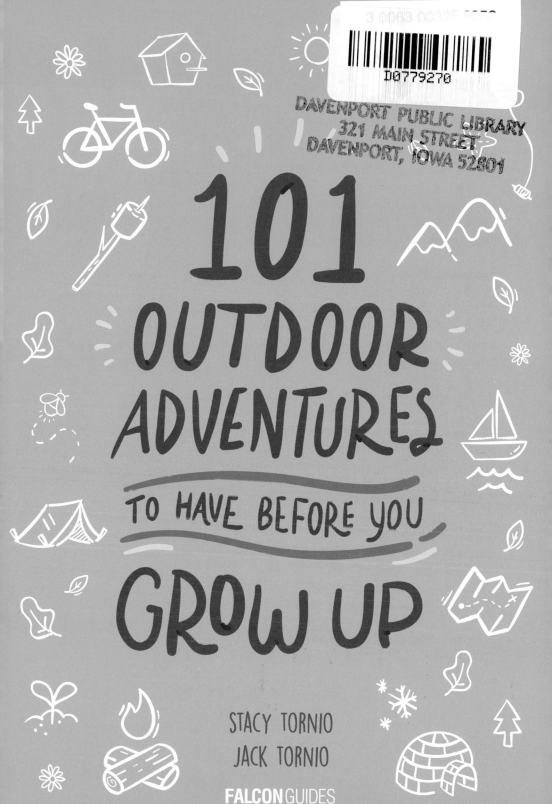

101 OUTDOOR ADVENTURES

TO HAVE BEFORE YOU

GROW UP

STACY TORNIO

JACK TORNIO

FALCONGUIDES

GUILFORD, CONNECTICUT

FALCONGUIDES®

An imprint of The Rowman & Littlefield Publishing Group, Inc.
4501 Forbes Blvd., Ste. 200
Lanham, MD 20706
www.rowman.com
Falcon and FalconGuides are registered trademarks and Make Adventure Your
Story is a trademark of The Rowman & Littlefield Publishing Group, Inc.

Distributed by NATIONAL BOOK NETWORK

Illustrations by Charity Ekpo

British Library Cataloguing in Publication Information available

Library of Congress Cataloging-in-Publication Data
Names: Tornio, Stacy, author. | Ekpo, Charity, illustrator.
Title: 101 outdoor adventures to have before you grow up / Stacy Tornio and
    Jack Tornio ; illustrations by Charity Ekpo.
Other titles: One hundred one outdoor adventures to have before you grow up
    | One Hundred and one outdoor adventures to have before you grow up |
    Falcon guide.
Description: Guilford, Connecticut : FalconGuides, [2019] | "Distributed by
    NATIONAL BOOK NETWORK"—T.p. verso.
Identifiers: LCCN 2018054309 (print) | LCCN 2018058968 (ebook) |
    ISBN 9781493041411 (Electronic) | ISBN 9781493041404 | ISBN
    9781493041404 (paperback : alk. paper) | ISBN 9781493041411 q(e-book)
Subjects: LCSH: Outdoor recreation.
Classification: LCC GV191.6 (ebook) | LCC GV191.6 .T67 2019 (print) | DDC
    796.5—dc23
LC record available at https://lccn.loc.gov/2018054309

∞™ The paper used in this publication meets the minimum requirements of
American National Standard for Information Sciences—Permanence of Paper
for Printed Library Materials, ANSI/NISO Z39.48-1992.

Printed in the United States of America

We dedicate this book to all the dogs out there who also love going outside. We hope you get the chance to take your pups out on adventures, too. And a special shout-out to our dogs—Payton, Daisy Mae, and Boomer.

SPECIAL THANKS

We want to give a special thanks to our family, especially Steve and Annabelle, for supporting us while writing this book.

A big, huge thanks to our editor, Katie Benoit, for seeing the vision of this book and helping us shape it. You made it better every step of the way. Another thanks to our agent, Uwe Stender, who immediately said, "This is a great idea," and always believes in us.

In the busy, digital world that we currently live in, it's not easy to make time for nature and getting outside. We thank everyone who helps us and encourages us to do this every single day. We hope you have the same and are able to do that for others, too.

CONTENTS

TRAVELING

BIKING

WILDLIFE WATCHING

FISHING

BACKYARDING

WATER ADVENTURING

MOUNTAINEERING

BEACHING

WINTERING

COOKING

CREATING

FOREWORD

When I was a kid, the outdoors was my playground, and I loved every minute.

I'd spend endless hours exploring the swamps and forests behind my house, searching for animals, collecting rocks, and building campfires. In spring and summer, I grew flowers and vegetables. In the fall, my father and I would search for berries and wild grapes for jam-making. Winter was all about sledding and snowmen. And of course, whether the available materials were logs, rocks, or snow, I was building forts.

When school got out, the family would pile in the car and drive out to explore the national parks. We hiked the Grand Canyon, explored the ancient Native American ruins of Mesa Verde, and tried our hands panning for gold in Yosemite.

But whatever the season, the outdoors was a source of endless wonder and limitless curiosity. There was just so much to know, and so much to explore. Whether I was tracking animals, trying to grow the biggest pumpkins, or building an igloo, I was asking questions, investigating, experimenting, and learning by doing.

In retrospect, I guess it's not a big surprise that I became a scientist. The outdoors trained me well. It taught me how to become fascinated, and how to explore, both physically and intellectually. Sharing the wonder about the natural world, through teaching, writing, and my YouTube channel, has become my life's passion.

Sadly, as I grew up, I realized that few of my peers had the chance to explore nature and come to love it. Everyone should have this opportunity, but it can be hard to know where to start. Stacy and Jack Tornio's book is a fabulous, accessible guide to getting outside and into nature. No matter where you live, or what your comfort level with the outdoors, there's something in here that will hook you, and I guarantee you'll be coming back for more.

When kids and their parents explore nature together, it can have a special way of building cross-generational bonds. In that regard, it's particularly cool that this book was written by a mother-and-son team. Stacy gives the informational overview, and Jack gives you a kid's tips and perspectives. New to the outdoors? They'll walk you through it together.

I had so much nostalgia reading through the excellent selection of activities in this book. Nonetheless, I still can't skip a rock ten times, haven't seen the northern lights, and haven't yet done a century ride. I guess that's a good reminder that, whatever our age, we've still got some exploring left to do.

Tyler DeWitt
YouTube Educator and Scientist

INTRODUCTION

How Does This Book Work?

Above all, we hope this book inspires you to get outside. There's no right or wrong way to use it. For instance, you might set out to conquer an entire chapter in a weekend, or these items could take you weeks, months, or years. In fact, we recommend not rushing it! Take your time and truly experience each checklist item as you go.

Every single thing in this book is totally achievable by you. Yes, you might have to travel to conquer some of the adventures. And it could take you some time. But we want this book to push your limits and even be challenging along the way.

For each item on the list, we broke it down into five easy steps. No, you don't have to do the steps in order. Instead, think of them as a guide as you go. These are the most important things to keep in mind as you set out to conquer each adventure.

You'll also want to look for Jack's Top Tips and Takeaways as you go. These are directly from Jack, offering a kid's perspective. He's always been an outdoorsy kid, and he has good advice from all the time he's spent outside.

Now even though we wrote this book for you—especially for kids—we hope you consider sharing it, too. All the items in this book can also be tackled as a family. Just open it up, pick something from the list, and go!

Please consider sharing your adventures with us along the way. Our Facebook page is Destination Nature, and our Instagram handle is TheDestinationNature. We'd love to see photos and get your tips, too. Now get out there and start checking things off your list.

Happy adventuring!

Stacy & Jack

A Note from Jack

What if a kid's book actually had a kid perspective in it? This is the question my mom and I asked when we talked about writing this book together. And it's exactly what we set out to do.

This book is for every kid out there who loves adventure and going outside. I know there's a lot of focus on getting toddlers and little kids outside to show them the natural world, and this is great. You have to start kids at a young age. But we specifically wrote this book for older kids—for you.

One of my main motivations for writing this book is that I'm a huge nature kid. I love climbing and exploring outside, and I always want nature to be part of my life. Some of the items were inspired by things I've already done, and many more are inspired by things I want to do. Yes, there are lots of things left on my list to tackle. For example, I haven't done nearly enough exploring around the mountains.

So, you might be wondering how we came up with the list. My mom and I talked about every single item on the list before we ever started writing. With each one, I'd think about it and whether it would be something I'd want to do—and whether it was challenging enough. Not everything made the final cut, but we're pretty happy with where we ended up. We hope it inspires you to get outside on your own or with family and friends. There's a lot to do before you grow up!

Jack

"IN EVERY WALK WITH NATURE, ONE RECEIVES FAR MORE THAN HE SEEKS."

—JOHN MUIR

Once you start hiking, you realize that it helps you explore the world in a whole new way. No matter where you travel, you can always find hiking paths nearby. And when you move away from the sidewalk, you'll see things you never imagined.

1
LEARN HOW TO BUILD A GOOD CAMPFIRE.

THE ART OF BUILDING A GOOD CAMPFIRE is something everyone should learn. It's not as easy as you'd think, either! Sure, you can just throw a bunch of sticks and wood together and light a match, but if you don't have the right shape and design, then it will go out quickly. Now, it might take a little bit of practice and patience, but it's definitely worth it. Eventually, you'll be able to build the perfect fire with flames that make amazing s'mores every single time.

1 To start with, make sure you have the right kind of wood and kindling. You'll want some good, solid firewood. You'll always want to gather some kindling—small twigs and sticks that will really help get things started. Ideally, use small pieces, 2 to 3 feet long. You don't want these starter pieces to be too thick. Save those pieces for when your fire is going strong. Finally, it's good to have some recycled paper products—cardboard, newspaper, or other papers—to use as well.

2 Start by crumpling up your paper or tearing it into small bits. For instance, if you have cardboard, shred it into strips. Put about half of this material down into the base of the fire location—such as in a fire ring or other designated and approved site.

3 Next, arrange your logs so that they overlap, making a tepee effect as you stack them upward. You probably need only three to five logs. Now tuck your kindling between your logs, along with scraps of your paper, too. Only use what you need—prepping your fire *too* much can actually do more harm than good. You want to leave a little bit of space between all the pieces so the air can circulate and the fire can get off to a good start.

4 Time to light it up! Whether you use matches or a lighter, you want to start by lighting the centermost and lowest part of the fire. This will allow those flames to work outward and upward, giving your fire the best chance to get a good start.

5 Now this is where you have to be careful. Don't just light your fire and then walk away. Stay there and patiently monitor it. If it's starting to catch but then you see it die down, add more kindling or paper. If it's a tiny little start, you might want to lean down and blow on it a bit. No matter what, don't give up on it. You'll get there with a little practice.

Jack's Top Tips and Takeaways

- **Pick a good place to build.** The space should be clear of extra materials, like garbage or other debris. You also want the space to be big enough so that the sparks won't ignite a fire in an area you don't want.

- **Have a good fire-poking stick.** This stick has to be long enough so that you can reach the fire without getting burned, but also short enough that you're comfortable moving it around. Metal sticks can be a good idea because they won't burn.

- **Don't try to go big too soon.** You don't need to waste all of your wood right away trying to create a big fire. Start out with small amounts of wood and add more once the fire is established at a higher temperature.

2
SET UP A TENT IN LESS THAN 15 MINUTES.

ONCE YOU LEARN HOW TO PITCH A TENT, you'll always have a roof over your head. Of course, anyone can set up a tent if there is an infinite amount of time, but it's really difficult to set it up in only 15 minutes. Speedy tent pitching is a good skill to have, though, especially if it's about to rain. Take a deep breath because this one might take a couple of tries to master.

1 Remove all the tent parts and supplies from the box or bag. You'll want to do a cross-check to make sure everything is there. This is an important step because it's really difficult to put a tent together if something is missing. Look for the instruction sheet that comes with your tent because it will help guide you through all of the parts.

2 Lay your tent flat on the ground where you want to set it up. Put your tent poles together, one end after the other, forming the backbone of your tent.

3 Slide the poles through the designated holes (again, let your instructions be your guide). Once all your poles are through, secure your tent to the ground with stakes, using a hammer or mallet, section by section. Imagine the tent as a big balloon, like the ones you see at parades, starting to inflate as you secure one section at a time.

4 Once you have all your areas secured, don't forget to add the rain flap. Yes, this still counts within your 15-minute time limit. Secure the flap with stakes and a mallet.

5 Finally, climb inside and test it out. For a comfortable rest, lay down a sleeping pad before you put your sleeping bag down. Once you're in and everything looks good, you can stop your timer to see if you met your goal.

Jack's Top Tips and Takeaways

- **Find a comfy surface.** You don't want to sleep on a surface that will hurt your back because of all the bumps on the ground. You also don't want to sleep on a slope because you might slide to the bottom of the tent. Find somewhere that's flat and smooth.

- **Cut yourself a break.** Not everyone is a natural. So if it is hard to set up a tent in under 15 minutes, practice. This is the key to success.

- **Imagine it first.** This might seem like odd advice, but it's good. Try to visualize what you have to do before you do it. Believe it or not, it will make it easier.

3

SLEEP OUTSIDE UNDER THE STARS.

SLEEPING UNDER THE STARS IN A TENT is always a great outdoors activity, but it's a whole other experience when you don't have a roof over your head. This is exactly what this challenge is about. Move out of the comfort of your tent and sleep under the stars.

1 Pick your approach. Are you going to put a sleeping bag near the campfire? Are you going to set up a tent hammock between two trees? Decide how you want to tackle this task. And don't be afraid to recruit a friend or family member to join you. It'll make it fun, and it'll be less intimidating this way.

2 Set up a tent. Wait a minute . . . aren't you supposed to skip the tent? This is true, but tents still make a good home base. You can put all your supplies inside, and, just in case the weather isn't great, you'll have somewhere to go.

3 Have a backup plan. It might seem intimidating at first to sleep outside completely in the open air. You'll probably worry about the weather or wild animals. Even though these are pretty small concerns, you should still know what to do about them. To avoid animals, make sure all your food is put away. This is the top thing that will attract animals. For bad weather, make sure you have access to shelter.

4 Check the weather, and pick a good time for your night under the stars. This will be the single best thing you can do to ensure you have a good experience. Look for a clear night so you get a good view of the stars and constellations.

5 Be sure to get all your supplies and equipment set up before it gets dark. Then sit back, relax, and enjoy the experience. Notice all the sounds of animals around you. Let the sounds of the crickets and cicadas fade into the background and help you fall asleep.

Jack's Top Tips and Takeaways

- **Challenge yourself to find the North Star.** It's one of the brightest stars in the sky, and it's a good challenge to try to find it on your own. Once you do find it, it'll help you find other constellations, too.

- **Don't set up under a bunch of trees.** To get the best experience, you want to have a nice, open view of the sky.

4
INVENT YOUR OWN S'MORES.

S'MORES ARE A STAPLE when you go camping. They're ooey, gooey, and a must-eat treat when you're sitting around the fire at night. Sure, most people know that you need graham crackers, marshmallows, and chocolate bars for s'mores, but this isn't the only way to eat them. Try coming up with your own style instead.

1 Dream it up, and do the research. There's really nothing that would be off limits for this one. If you like it, then try it. Some ideas might include using wafers instead of graham crackers, Nutella instead of a milk chocolate bar, and strawberries or bananas as an extra add-on.

2 Once you've thought of some typical options, be a little daring next. Cheese on s'mores? Sure, give it a try. Pickles? Hmm, if you're brave enough, go for it. Really challenge yourself to think outside of the box. Maybe you'll come up with something amazing!

3 Your recipe can have anything you want, but you'll still want to roast the perfect marshmallow for your s'more. The trick to a perfect roasting is to be patient. Avoid the temptation to dip your marshmallow into the flame and set it on fire. This won't really cook it all that well. Instead, hold it above the coals (not the flames) and wait it out.

4 Lay out all your ingredients so they're ready to go as soon as the marshmallow comes off the fire. Stack them up, one after another. Then take a bite of your masterpiece.

5 What works? What doesn't? All good chefs tweak their recipes until they are happy with them. This is part of the process. Don't be afraid to change things up and keep testing s'mores recipes until you get it just right. Then when you do, take a picture, write down your ingredients, and share your recipe with others. This kind of goodness shouldn't be kept to yourself.

Jack's Top Tips and Takeaways

- **Focus on ingredients you like.** If you try to make a really creative or weird s'more but you don't like it, then what's the point? Start off with things you love. Personally, my favorite candy is Reese's so I would probably do something with Reese's tucked in.

- **Have a friendly little competition.** Competing against the people you love is the best. To go along with that, s'mores are one of the best foods ever. Why not combine the two to create one of the greatest things of all time?

- **Borrow some ideas from online.** Some people struggle with being creative. But everyone might want to do this challenge. So if they're stuck for recipes, have them look up ideas using ingredients they like.

5

COOK AN ENTIRE MEAL OVER THE CAMPFIRE.

YOU'VE PROBABLY ALREADY CONQUERED hot dogs and s'mores, but have you ever cooked an entire meal over the campfire? For this challenge, really test yourself and go outside of your comfort zone to make something a little more difficult or unique.

1 Decide what you're going to have for an appetizer. You can go online to look up good campfire recipes. You'll probably find that there are entire websites and books dedicated to amazing campfire recipes. A good appetizer might include roasted veggies with cheese, toasted nuts, or even a bruschetta (toasted bread with salsa or diced tomatoes on top). You can easily make any of these by preparing them and baking them in foil.

2 Decide what you're going to have for a main dish. Don't be tempted to just go with hot dogs. You can do better than that. Try shish kabobs with your favorite meat stacked with veggies. Other good options might include burgers, grilled cheese, or mini pizzas.

3 Decide what to have for dessert. There are so many desserts you can make in foil over an open flame. Try making your own popcorn and then drizzle it with chocolate sauce. Other campfire desserts might include making miniature cherry pies with bread or creating cinnamon and sugar bites using cinnamon, sugar, and pieces of bread.

4 Place all of the ingredients for your meal over the fire. If the ingredients are difficult to carry or take along, consider putting them in individual containers to make it easier. (At-home prep on some of these recipes is key.) Don't forget aluminum foil. It really is a great trick for cooking over the campfire.

5 Assign your fellow campers some jobs, and let the meal prep begin. You'll probably need some extra hands to help with cooking your campfire meal. Someone needs to tend to the fire, making sure it has good coals for cooking. Another person can help with meal prep or organizing so the food's ready to go on right away. Cook and eat as you go!

Jack's Top Tips and Takeaways

- **It might be hard to cook over the fire without the necessary materials.** Cooking over the fire is never easy, but you can make it easier by having the right equipment to cook. Look for special supplies by searching "camping cookware" on Amazon.

- **Eggs are a go-to favorite.** Eggs are very good to eat if you don't have a lot of time or you need energy in a small package. They have good protein, they don't take a lot of time, and you can make them in many different ways.

- **Practice at home.** You may want to practice making meals over the fire in your backyard so you don't burn your food when it comes time to cook over a campfire.

6

CAMP OFF THE GRID.

IF YOU'VE CAMPED AT A POPULAR CAMPGROUND, then you know how busy it can get. During the summer, the campsites will easily sell out, and you'll find yourself very close to your neighbor. If you're the type of person who likes a little alone time and privacy, then say goodbye to the popular sites and go off the grid instead. It's an experience everyone should try at least once.

1 First, find a great campground. If you've never camped off the grid, you might not know where to start looking. If you google "campground" in an area that you're looking at, chances are you'll find the typical (and busy) options. So, instead, start asking around to friends and family that you know like to camp. They'll be able to point you in the right direction.

2 Don't be afraid to hike a little extra to find the perfect location. If you truly want to be in an area where others aren't, you might have to be willing to hike a few miles to get to your site. Explore your favorite park or wildlife area to see if you can get to a secluded location by hiking to it instead of driving.

3 Check for rules and regulations. If it's truly a remote location, it might not have any rules at all. But for those locations that are still official but more remote, look up their reservation system. A lot of times, these types of sites are "first come, first served," so it pays to get there early.

4 Prepare for a different kind of camping experience. You probably won't have water or bathrooms nearby for easy access, so keep this in mind when you're packing. In addition, you'll want to make sure you think ahead to pack the right amount of food and other supplies.

5 Get out and enjoy your time camping off the grid. Notice how the stars seem brighter and the sounds at night are even louder. You might be a bit surprised at first at just how quiet it is, but once you get used to it, it's a really amazing experience.

Jack's Top Tips and Takeaways

- **Ask around to get the best secret spots.** Locals are the best people to ask. So, if you're in a new area and don't know where to go, stop off at a coffee shop or an outdoors store to see if the locals there might know a good spot.

- **Don't leave your trash.** Wild animals don't need your food. Bring an extra bag of some sort or something to keep the garbage out of the wild. One way to remember to take the garbage with you is, "Pack it in, and pack it out."

- **Look for sites near water.** You won't be the only person who thinks of this, but these are some of the best areas. Plus this can give you fresh water, a way to stay clean, and a source of food.

7
CREATE YOUR OWN CAMPFIRE SONG.

GET YOUR VOICE READY because everyone needs to experience the fun of singing around the campfire. This is a tradition that has been around for years, and you really don't have to be that good of a singer to enjoy it. All you need is a little creativity and a tune that you already know. This will make it easier to come up with your own song!

1 Pick a tune that you know. If you're working on this song with a friend or family member, pick a song that everyone is familiar with. For instance, "Twinkle, Twinkle, Little Star" is a good one. You could also pick a favorite song that's on the radio.

2 Choose a section of the song, and then write new words to match. For instance, "Twinkle Twinkle, Little Star" might become something like, "Twinkle, Twinkle, Big Bright Fire." Take one line at a time, rewriting it to tell a story or show your love for camping and the outdoors.

3 Practice your song a few times. Write down all the words and have them on standby in case you forget some. You don't need music for the song, unless someone you know plays guitar, and that's always a good idea around the fire. Instead, just sing a capella or have some people help you out by humming the tune.

4 Get ready for the campfire show. Wait, there's a show? Having a campfire talent show is a great way to spend the night at your campsite. You can have a theme like everyone sings a song. Or you can have people choose all different talents to show off.

5 Belt it out! Singing your own song around the campfire shouldn't be whispered. No way. You spent time and your creative energy on those words, so you want to make sure they get heard. You might even want to record it so you have it to play back.

Jack's Top Tips and Takeaways

- **Songs don't always need instruments.** Some songs are good because of all the different voices or tones used in a verse or song. A lot of campfire songs include the use of guitars or other instruments, but your voice is the best instrument. (Humming in the background is good, too.)

- **The song doesn't need to be written out.** The most important part about a campfire song is having fun while singing it. Sometimes it doesn't need to make sense or sound good; you just need to have fun while singing it.

8

CAMP IN A HAMMOCK.

TECHNICALLY, YOU COULD FULFILL the Sleeping under the Stars adventure by also doing this list item. Hammock camping is a wonderful way to sleep outside under the stars. This is a very popular hobby right now, so you'll find lots of hammock options that are meant for nighttime camping. You could also just try a backyard hammock if you're adventurous, and if you don't have to worry about mosquitoes.

1 Find a good hammock. With so many tent hammocks out there, you'll have plenty of options to choose from. Hit up your local sports or outdoors store to see if they have any on display that you can try out for yourself. You don't necessarily need things like a mosquito net on top or a pillow, but they might be really nice to have.

2 Test out your hammock. It might seem like there's not much setup with a tent hammock, but you still have to unpack it, set it up the right way, and learn how to secure the ends around trees. You don't want to come crashing down at night!

3 Give it a trial run. Go through all the steps of setting up your hammock properly, and then give it a test by taking an afternoon nap. Challenge yourself to completely do this on your own instead of having a parent or someone else do it for you.

4 Look for the perfect place to set up your tent hammock for a night of camping. Again, the right set of trees can

make a big difference. You might have found a good set in your own backyard, but you'll have a new challenge if you take your hammock with you on a trip. Remember what you learned in your testing stage, and apply those same rules when you're looking for a new location.

5 Get in, zip up, and relax! A lot of people like hammock camping because it's comfortable. There's no knobby or rocky ground to lie on. You're just hanging in the air, and breathing in that fresh outdoor air.

Jack's Top Tips and Takeaways

- **Keep a flashlight nearby.** Sometimes you might have to get up in the middle of the night for a variety of reasons . . . like going to the bathroom. A flashlight will definitely come in handy.

- **Look for an even area.** If you want to sleep well throughout the night, make sure your hammock is even. You don't want one side a lot higher than the other because you might slide down, which is not comfortable.

- **Have protection from bugs, rain, and other conditions.** If you don't have a mosquito net, you might end up with dozens of red, itchy bumps all over your body the next morning. If you don't have a cover above your hammock, you might wake up soaked. So just check the weather and your gear. I have made this mistake before, and it's no fun to be itchy and wet.

9

TRY ULTRALIGHT CAMPING.

HAVE YOU HEARD OF ULTRALIGHT CAMPING? It's pretty much exactly how it sounds—it's camping with really light gear that doesn't weigh you down. This isn't as easy as it sounds. Camping gear naturally tends to be a little bit heavy and bulky, and that's because you want it to be sturdy. So if you try ultralight camping, you might need to look for new supplies or borrow some for this challenge.

1 The reason people do ultralight camping is because they're usually hiking, biking, or canoeing. There's a reason they want to keep their gear light—they don't have a lot of space or they're going to a fairly remote destination. Pick a place you want to go where you'd need to bring an ultralight pack.

2 Start packing, weighing, and putting your backpack to the test. You'll want to set a goal of how light you want your pack to be. Try to make it half as heavy as it would normally be. So, for instance, if your backpack is usually 30 pounds, try to get it down to 15 pounds instead.

3 Go through your pack one final time, and challenge yourself to get rid of everything you don't need. If you're able to shave a couple more pounds off, this will really help as you're trekking through the woods or canoeing down a river.

4 Secure your pack to your bike, canoe, or yourself so it won't wiggle or fall. If you're canoeing or kayaking, make sure all your supplies have waterproof protection, too.

5 As you try ultralight camping, keep track as you go of what works and what doesn't. Are there supplies you didn't use at all? Were there things you wish you had? Adjust as you go, and do what works for you.

Jack's Top Tips and Takeaways

- **Protect your valuables.** You don't want to lose, break, or damage your phone or any other valuables you have along during the trip. One way to keep that from happening is to keep them in a small bag. If it's waterproof, that's even better.

- **Try small packages.** To save space, bring food in small containers. You might have to unpack things from typical bags or containers and repack them into smaller ones to make the most of your space.

- **Share space.** If you are camping with multiple people, compare notes and share the space. Not only is this nice, but it's efficient. You don't duplicate items. Then your space will go a lot further.

GARDENING

"TO PLANT A GARDEN IS TO BELIEVE IN TOMORROW."

—AUDREY HEPBURN

A lot of people tend to be intimidated by gardening. They'll say, "Oh, I don't have a green thumb," or "I kill everything I plant." Don't let yourself believe this. Even if you've had bad luck with plants in the past, give it another try. It really isn't all that difficult.

From growing veggies to flowers, there are really just two basics to keep in mind to have gardening success. First of all, give your plants sunshine. This is important—they need light to grow. Second of all, don't forget to water. This is one of the most difficult activities to keep up because life gets busy and you just forget sometimes, but if you can master it, you're pretty much guaranteed to have success with gardening.

10
PLANT A BIRD AND BUTTERFLY GARDEN.

IF YOU'RE GOING TO PLANT A GARDEN, why not attract birds and butterflies at the same time? All it takes is a little bit of planning. Flowers such as milkweed, coneflower, and aster can bring wildlife to your area.

1 Learn what plants are best for your area. To do this, start by talking to a local gardener you know and trust. Or hit up the local garden center to ask the workers. They love giving recommendations. You can also look into your area native plant society. Just google it or "nature plans for _____" to get good recommendations. The reasons native plants are so good is that they have already been established in your area. This makes them naturally attractive to birds and butterflies.

2 Now narrow down that plant list. It's so easy to get overwhelmed by all these plants you want to grow, but you have to be realistic about what you have space for. Focus on whether you need plants for sun, shade, or a mix of both, and this will help you decide. Try to start with just a few plants, unless you have a big space to fill.

3 Know the right time of year to plant. Spring is almost always a good time to plant, but fall can be a good time as well. You can easily research specific planting times by type of plant.

4 Either buy the plants or start them from seed. If you're looking for quicker results, then plants are the way to go. Look for plant sales (especially through native plant organizations) that might be happening in your area. This is a good way to get milkweed (great for monarch butterflies) and native coneflowers (perfect for birds). Be sure to follow the label or directions for each plant to have the greatest chance of success.

5 Don't forget to water and take care of your plants. This is probably the number one mistake gardeners make. They forget to water, and the plants suffer. Don't let this be you. Plants especially need extra water when they're trying to get established. So put watering on your calendar.

Jack's Top Tips and Takeaways

- **Milkweed is good for monarch butterflies, so plant some.** Milkweed is the host plant for monarchs. This means the monarch caterpillars need it for food. It should definitely be part of your planting plan.

- **Pineapple sage is a good plant for hummingbirds.** This is one of my all-time favorite plants because it smells good. Hummingbirds like it because it has red blooms (they like the color red) and it has good nectar inside.

- **You only need a few perennials to get started.** This is because each and every perennial plant you grow will get bigger each year. Also, the plant will drop seeds and multiply. So if there is a little bit of open space in your garden, just leave it that way because it will probably fill in over the years.

11

LEARN THE DIFFERENCE BETWEEN FLOWERS AND WEEDS.

IT'S EASY TO KNOW WHAT THE LEAVES of a specific flower look like when you first plant it. But when it's not in bloom, it can be pretty tricky to differentiate it from a weed. This is especially true in spring when leaves are just starting to emerge. You'll look at it and wonder if it's a weed (pull it) or a flower (leave it). Even the best of gardeners make mistakes in knowing what's a weed or a flower, so this is a pretty difficult task to master. But here are some tips to make it easier.

1 Notice three basic things when you come across a plant that you're unsure about. First, look at the leaves and note the size and shape of them. Next, look at the stem and how the leaves are attached. Is there a single big one? Several small ones? Finally, notice if it looks a lot bigger than other plants around it. Weeds naturally tend to grow faster and be more aggressive than plants. So if it's much bigger, it might be a sign that it's a weed.

2 When it's in bloom, take a picture of your plant. Try to take a close-up picture of the leaves, especially how they are attached to the stem. This will help you with an ID.

3 Start your search online, looking up some of the most common backyard weeds. The *Farmer's Almanac* has a great article on its website, almanac.com, called "Common Garden Weed." This article has a good overview of weeds, and it pictures the twelve most common ones. Does your mystery plant look like any of these?

4 Are you still questioning if the plant is a weed or a flower? Consider an identification app. You'll find plenty of flower/weed options, so you could learn to identify your plant with just the swipe of your finger. There are even apps where you can submit a picture, and the app will help you identifiy the plant based off the image. We particularly like the Leafsnap app. If apps aren't cutting it, hit up your local library and check out a plant and weed book. Chances are, your library will have a few good resources for your area.

5 Now that you've learned to identify weeds, it's time to get rid of them. Don't let them stay in your garden, taking water and nutrients from your other plants. Get them out of there, and keep your garden weeded so that your other plants can thrive.

Jack's Top Tips and Takeaways

- Getting rid of weeds is much easier after a rainfall. This is because the soil will be soft and wet so it is easier to pull longer roots out of the ground.

- Just because a plant has flowers doesn't mean it's not a weed. A lot of weeds have flowers. Bindweed, chickweed, pigweed, and dandelions are just some of them. A lot of these plants aren't harmful to you, but they take away important nutrients from your other plants.

- Talk to an expert. Sometimes it's hard to learn what's a weed and what's a flower based on the internet. Don't be afraid to seek the help of an expert who can give you better advice in person.

12
GROW YOUR OWN HERBS.

LOVE COOKING? YOU DEFINITELY WANT to learn how to grow your own herbs. If you do, you'll always have fresh flavor in the dishes that you make. You can grow herbs both inside and outside, so this is a challenge you can knock out pretty much any time of the year.

1 Learn about different types of herbs. Find out what the top herbs are for your favorite dishes you like to cook. Basil, rosemary, and parsley are common basic herbs to get you started. You can use these for several dishes, and they're pretty easy to grow.

2 To begin, stick to growing herbs in a container. Choose a good container and a quality soil mix. You don't need a huge container—6 inches deep (or more) is good. You can find good container soil mix in the soil section of your garden center. Don't just use soil from your backyard.

3 Set up your herbs in a sunny location. Almost all herbs do best in full sun, so you want to find a good location if you want to have long-term success.

4 Keep the containers watered, but don't overwater. If you're growing herbs inside, you'll probably see them on a regular basis, so it'll remind you to water more. But don't overdo it. Just feel the top layer of soil with your fingers, and if it still feels moist, skip it until later.

5 Don't be afraid to harvest your herbs when they're small. Herbs aren't like other veggies where you need to wait 60, 90, or more days. You can harvest leaves from herbs within a few weeks or even sooner if you're starting with established plants. The herbs can even be more flavorful during this time.

Jack's Top Tips and Takeaways

- **Stay away from drafty windows.** Herbs can't live well in the cold or in temperatures that vary a lot. This is why if you grow herbs in the winter, you should make sure they get good sunlight (usually by a window), but you don't want it to be too drafty. This could freeze the plant.

- **Herbs can come and go quickly.** It can seem like your herb plants don't last long or you just use the herbs quickly. If you want them to last longer, keep planting seeds or plants so you'll be able to have fresh herbs all year.

- **Look for other ways to use herbs.** A lot of herbs are good for seasoning in your favorite dish, but you might also want to save or dry them. For instance, you could also pick off mint or pineapple sage to make a tea. Other herbs can be dried and stored until you're ready to use them.

13

TRY GROWING A GARDEN IN A BOX.

DID YOU KNOW THAT ALL YOU NEED for a successful garden is a cardboard box? It's true. Now that box from your latest online shopping trip can be turned into a miniature garden, making it perfect for growing veggies.

1 Find a good, strong box for your garden. You don't need it to be particularly big or bulky. In fact, you don't want it too big because you will be filling it with soil, and then it will get too heavy. A good box size to try would be a 12-inch square.

2 Fill your box with good soil, just as you'd do with a garden container. Look at the garden center for a soil mix specifically made for containers. This will give you a greater chance of success.

3 Add your plant or plants. Keep in mind that this is like growing in containers, so you have to limit how much can go in each container. A 12-inch-square box would be good for either a single tomato or pepper plant or about four lettuce plants or twelve carrots. Another great thing to grow in your cardboard box is potatoes.

4 Water your plants just like you usually would. At first you might be worried about the cardboard box holding up, but you'll see that it's actually pretty sturdy. Even with water or rain, it should hold its shape.

5 When your plants are ready to harvest, pick them or harvest as you normally would. For potatoes, it's really fun because you can actually tear the box completely apart to find the potatoes instead of having to dig them up. Then put your cardboard in the recycling bin, and start over again with a new box.

Jack's Top Tips and Takeaways

- **Dress it up.** Cardboard boxes are pretty plain. Make the box look pretty by adding designs, painting it, or even putting burlap around it.

- **A shoebox is great for growing herbs.** Herbs don't need that much room, so try using a shoebox. It's sturdy and portable. If you don't have any shoeboxes, then maybe you should go to the store and buy some shoes. Because sometimes you just have to *treat yourself*!

14

GROW YOUR OWN TOMATOES.

TOMATOES ARE THE MOST POPULAR homegrown veggie for backyard gardeners. There are hundreds of different types you can grow, from the traditional red to yellow, orange, black, and even green. Once you learn the basics of growing tomatoes, you can then apply that knowledge to growing many other veggies.

1 Study up on the different types of tomatoes. The first thing to consider is your desired size and shape. If you want smaller and bite-size, look for cherry tomatoes. Looking for a little bit bigger? Look for plum tomato options. And there are plenty of options for the bigger, more traditional-looking tomatoes. You don't have to select just one type to grow—try them all! But this is your first step.

2 Now that you understand the different tomato types a bit more, look at specific varieties. This is where you'll find hundreds and hundreds of options. Read about each one—they often have cool names—and the description will tell you about the taste, how long it takes to grow them, and more details. You'll naturally be drawn to some more than others. Choose whichever one sounds good to you.

3 Pick the right location for your tomatoes. The area needs to have good soil and great sunshine, and it should be an area that you see regularly. This is for good reason—it'll help you remember to water.

4 If you're growing multiple varieties, plant your tomato plants at least a foot apart. You'll want to put a tomato cage around them right away—you can find one at your local gardening center. Or if you're not going to cage them, tie them up to a trellis. This way as the plants grow, they'll grow into the cage or trellis.

5 Keep the area around your tomatoes weeded. This will help your tomatoes grow and develop. In addition, keep them watered. In the heat of the summer, you really should water them every single day. Finally, enjoy. If you have a good season, you'll probably have more tomatoes than you know what to do with. Have fun making and enjoying different tomato dishes to come up with creative ways to eat them all.

Jack's Top Tips and Takeaways

- **A single tomato plant doesn't need a lot of space.** You might think you need a ton of space for a tomato, but you don't. This means a small container or box will work just fine.

- **Fresh salsa and guacamole are really easy to make.** Next time you need a great dip for your chips, go to your garden. All you need are some tomatoes, peppers, onions, and cilantro to make a really basic salsa. For guacamole, all you need is a tomato, an avocado, fresh herbs such as cilantro, and whatever other spices you want to add.

15

PLANT SOMETHING FOR 5 YEARS FROM NOW.

GARDENING IS SUCH A REWARDING HOBBY, and many types of plants last for years. Think about the established gardens you see in your neighborhood and the trees and shrubs growing there. Those have often been growing for quite a while. So for this challenge, let's focus on growing a tree or shrub that will be around for the next 20, 50, or 100 years.

1 Identify the space first. This step might seem like it's out of order, but since you need a lot of room to grow trees and shrubs, you don't want to plant something there that is too big. This is actually a really common mistake. Gardeners will often plant a tree or shrub in an area that they want to fill, but they forget to look at the label to see that it grows 75 feet! This is why it's important to find the space first, and then look for the right tree or shrub to fill it.

2 Now you can go shopping for trees and shrubs. Once you've identified your space and you have a general idea of the size you need to fill it, look for the perfect fit. You can walk up and down the aisles of the garden center to start getting an idea of what you might want to grow (check the labels).

3 Once you've settled on the type of tree or shrub you want to grow, do a little more research. You thought you were done, right? Nope. There are so many options when it comes to different types of trees and shrubs (usually called cultivars). For instance, a dogwood comes in both tree and shrub options. And many others can vary a lot in size, color, and overall look, just based on different varieties. Read the entire label to learn light needs, size, and other important information before you purchase.

4 Now it's time to plant. With both trees and shrubs, a good rule of thumb is to dig a hole twice as big and deep as the root or rootball. (A rootball is how many trees are available to purchase. They are often wrapped in burlap or plastic because they were dug up from a tree farm and are now ready to be planted in your yard.)

5 In your tree or shrub's first year, stake it if necessary. (This means you'll give it extra support while it's small so the wind or weather doesn't whip it around.) Then give it lots of water that first year to help it get established. Then every year after that, keep an eye on it and give it extra attention as it needs it. You want to give your plant a lot of attention early on so it will live for many years.

Jack's Top Tips and Takeaways

- **Look for mini alternatives.** Sometimes you like trees or shrubs that are big or bulky, but you don't have the space. Don't worry. There are a lot of trees and shrubs that can come in a dwarf variety. This is usually just a smaller version of the original plant.

- **Document your progress.** Sometimes it's hard to remember when a tree or shrub started growing. Keep a log, with visuals, to track how much your tree or shrub has grown over the years.

16
DESIGN YOUR OWN GARDEN BED.

IF YOU'VE IMAGINED THE PERFECT GARDEN, then now is the time to put that plan into action. Anyone can be a garden designer. There are just a few basic tips to keep in mind, and then you can create your own garden getaway.

1 Tour lots of gardens. Let them be your teacher, and study what you like, what you don't like, and how the experienced gardeners have laid things out. You don't have to go to fancy or professional gardens either. Just going to the backyard of gardeners you know is also a good way to get different ideas. Public gardens, parks, and monuments also offer up some creative inspiration.

2 Learn the basics of size and shape. Almost all plants include instructions on the label about how tall and wide they grow. This is a great indicator of how many plants you might need in one area. You might think you need twenty or thirty plants in a garden, but once you realize how big they'll eventually grow, you might see that it's more like ten or fifteen plants.

3 Understand the basics of light needs. If you mix full-sun and full-shade plants together in a really shady location, you might have some challenges. As you plan your garden, check out the light needs of each and every plant you want to grow. Make sure you're grouping the right kinds of plants together, and make sure your planned area accounts for that type of light.

4 Put your plan down on paper. This is the final step before planting, but it's really important. Do a little sketch of how you envision your garden to look when it's all growing and blooming. This will help you figure out where to position each plant and how many of each you will need.

5 It's planting time! Make sure your garden bed is prepped and weed-free. Then plant according to your plan and the labels. Once they're all set, water right away. If you're planting directly into the ground and not in a raised bed or container, mulch the area afterward. This will help keep weeds away and preserve your water.

Jack's Top Tips and Takeaways

- **Borrow great designs.** Making a whole new design on your own is hard, but it's perfectly fine to tweak someone else's. Look online or ask for help from a friend.

- **Try container designing first.** If an entire garden bed intimidates you or you think it's too much, then start with containers. A lot of times you might not have the time or space to create a whole garden bed. A set of containers works great, too.

HIKING

"WILDERNESS IS NOT A LUXURY BUT NECESSITY OF THE HUMAN SPIRIT."

—EDWARD ABBEY

Hiking is just walking, right? Well . . . kinda . . . perhaps . . . maybe a little . . . no, not really at all. Hiking gives you the opportunity to explore nature in a whole new way. It allows you to go off the pavement to get up close with the outdoors.

Once you start hiking, you realize that it helps you explore the world with new eyes. No matter where you travel, you can always find hiking paths nearby. And when you move away from the sidewalk, you'll see things you never imagined.

≒ 17 ≒
GO ON AN AMAZING DAY HIKE.

HIKING IS ONE OF THE GREATEST WAYS to escape into nature. It's also a good way to explore your neighborhood, city, or a new area. You probably already hike, but if you haven't planned an all-day hiking adventure, now is the time. Make a plan to go solo or with friends, but it needs to be an all-day endeavor.

1 The first step for planning an amazing day hike is to pick a great nearby destination. A good day hike will likely be 5 to 7 miles. This might not sound like much at first, but remember that it usually takes a lot longer to hike on a trail than to walk or run the same distance on pavement. Challenge yourself a bit. Don't just hike a trail that is marked easy, but instead push yourself to do a moderate or even challenging one. Look at the calendar and pick a date that works with the weather.

2 After you've set your eyes on a trail and you've picked a date, be sure to put together a day pack. Choose lightweight snacks and food that will fuel your hiking throughout the day. Good options include fruit, nuts, and PB&Js. To save even more weight and space, use a day pack that has a built-in water reservoir.

3 It's time to hit the hiking trail! It's best to start early, especially if you're adventuring out during summer. This will also allow you some time flexibility so you don't feel rushed to finish before sunset.

4 During your hike, pace yourself. It's not a race or something to rush through. Part of having an amazing day hike is really taking the time to enjoy it. Breathe in the fresh air. Notice the signs of nature all around you. Take it all in. And don't forget to drink plenty of water and stop for snacks to energize along the way.

5 After you finish your day hike, write down notes about it. Was there a section you really loved? What did you see? You could even come up with your own rating system, and then rate all the hikes you go on so you have a record of past hikes when planning hikes in the future.

Jack's Top Tips and Takeaways

- **Take more water than you think you need.** The general recommendation is to drink about 2 liters a day. But don't be afraid to pack extra. Remember, your pack gets lighter as you drink water, so it's OK to start a little heavier.

- **Sneak in at least one sweet treat.** It's good to have healthy options, but sometimes when you're trying to get through a tough part of the trail, you need something else. My favorite is a Reese's Peanut Butter Cup. Gummy bears are a good option, too. Don't overdo it on the quick dose of sugar, but it's nice to have when you need some energy.

- **Have a plan in case you get lost.** It's easy to get turned around on the trail. Always have a backup plan to get yourself back on track.

18

CREATE AND COMPLETE YOUR OWN TRIATHLON.

MANY PEOPLE HAVE A LIFE GOAL of completing a big, monumental race like a half marathon, marathon, or a triathlon. This is because it takes a lot of time and training to pull it off. Ready to accomplish this goal now? Let's go!

1 Triathlons can come in many shapes and forms, so you first need to decide what type you want to conquer. Traditionally, triathlons are defined as a swimming, running, and biking event. The running can be hiking instead, but it's great to do it on the trail. If you want to replace biking or swimming, try kayaking or canoeing instead. It might not be a traditional triathlon, but it still counts!

2 Set a distance goal for each leg of your triathlon. A traditional triathlon (what they do in the Olympics, for example) is a swim of 1.5 kilometers (.93 mile), a bike ride of 40 kilometers (24.8 miles), and a 10-kilometer run (6.2 miles). Again, set your own goals. Maybe you want to do a half or mini triathlon instead. No matter what, be sure to challenge yourself. You don't want it to be easy.

3 Start your training plan. A good amount of training time is about 10 to 14 weeks before your triathlon. This gives you enough time to train about four to five days a week. You can easily find training plans online to follow, so you can mark off each day as you complete it. Or if you're doing your own plan, make up your own calendar. A good rule of thumb for a hiking, biking, and swimming triathlon would be doing each activity two or three times a week. This means you'll double up on some days, combining two activities.

4 Don't forget to include rest days as part of your training plan. Do have some physical activity, though, on those days. Go for a walk, stretch, try yoga, or do other low-impact activities. This will help you stay active and keep you moving.

5 The night before your race day, get a good night of sleep. On race day, be sure to drink lots of water, and don't be late to

your event. You might be tempted to go really hard or fast at first, but don't do this. You'll get tired too fast. Pace yourself so you don't run out of steam.

Jack's Top Tips and Takeaways

- **Bring on the competition.** If you love competition, look for official triathlon events in your area. Some triathlons will even have specific age divisions so you can see how you match up against your peers.

- **Do all parts of the training.** Make sure you have spent time training for each and every event. You will likely have a least favorite event because it's challenging for you. This might make you tempted to skip it or not practicie it as much, but don't. This is probably the event you should spend the most time training for.

- **Bribe yourself.** Yes, bribery works great for something like this. When you set a goal or a reward for yourself, you're definitely more likely to do it. Better yet, have your mom, dad, or another adult set a reward for you instead!

19
FIND A FOSSIL.

WHO DOESN'T WANT TO FIND A FOSSIL? It sounds awesome, right? Now you might think this is next to impossible, but it's really not. While most people think of a dinosaur bone when they hear the word fossil (and that would be pretty challenging to find), there are lots of other ways to find a fossil.

1. Know what a fossil is. This might seem like an obvious step, but it's an important one. While most people think of bones as true fossils, this is just one type. There are actually two types of fossil, including body and trace. Body fossils are parts of actual animals like teeth, bones, and shells. Trace fossils are signs of living things that include footprints, tracks, and impressions. They are easier to find in the wild.

2. Know where to find trace fossils. This is an important step because it'll make your fossil hunt a lot easier. Typically, you'll want to look for areas where rocks are breaking away and eroding. Water areas, cliffs, or other spots where the rocks are breaking away are all great options.

3. After you know where to look, it's important to know the type of rock to look for, too. You want to look for fossils in sedimentary rocks (sandstone, limestone, shale). These rocks are layered and have the best chance of being home to a fossil.

4. Finally, if you find a good area where it looks like there could be fossils, don't be afraid to get up close and personal. This

might mean crawling through some muddy areas or using a magnifying glass to look for small impressions or markings in the rock.

5 When you find a fossil, take a picture of it, but don't break it. You might be tempted to bust the rock apart to get it out, but don't. You could cause unnecessary damage, so leave it alone. You can always share your picture with a local geologist if you think you found something unique.

Jack's Top Tips and Takeaways

- **Look and learn.** If you are having a hard time figuring out what a fossil looks like, go on Google images and search for "trace fossil" to get a look at several options. This will help you get an idea of what you should be looking for when you go hunting.

- **Find water first.** One of the best places to find fossils is near bodies of water. This is because water naturally draws in animals. And, because water is constantly moving, it's always bringing new things to the surface.

20
HIKE TO ONE OF THE TALLEST POINTS IN YOUR STATE.

CLIMBING TO THE TOP OF A GIANT HILL, tower, or mountain is a big accomplishment. Plus the views are pretty amazing. You should be able to pull this one off in a single day or afternoon. You just need some good weather, and you'll be all set.

1 Set your sights on a goal. If you live in a state with lots of mountains, like Colorado or Washington, you might have to settle for a big hill instead of the tallest point in the whole state. (Seriously, it would be over 14,000 feet if you tried to climb a mountain!) A good goal is to find a high point to hike within an hour or two of your home. It should also be a point you can reach in a few hours.

2 Once you have your goal, do the research to make sure you know the best time to go, what the weather will be that day, and the right path to take. Ideally, you'll pick a day that's not too hot or cold. Otherwise, just make sure you dress for the weather and take layers in case you need to adjust as you go.

3 On the day of your big climb, pack plenty of water and snacks to keep you going throughout the day. Be careful you don't make your day pack too heavy.

4 Start your climb! If possible, start early in the morning to give yourself plenty of time to linger and stop to look at things. It will be more difficult going up than down, but you still want to pace yourself so you don't overdo it early in the day.

5 Once you reach the top, take in the view and enjoy your accomplishment. If you have a camera available, be sure to capture the moment.

Jack's Top Tips and Takeaways

- **Pick the right place for your skill level.** Make sure you don't pick something so easy it takes 10 minutes and you don't have to try. But you also don't want to pick a hike so hard it will take 10 hours. This way you can enjoy yourself the whole time.

- **Bring a combo of healthy snacks and treats.** Be sure to take plenty of food and water but don't pack a bunch of junk food that will make you have a sugar crash. Make sure to have healthy food along with just a little bit of a sugary snack.

- **Try a different season.** If you like the view of a place that you went to, check it out in a different season, too. It'll give you a whole new perspective depending on the time of year that you go.

21
MAKE A HIKING STICK, AND USE IT ON A HIKE.

YOU'VE PROBABLY SEEN PEOPLE using hiking sticks while going along a trail. They are particularly helpful to have when you're ascending or descending because they help you keep your balance. They can also give you that little extra bit of oomph you need to keep going. Instead of buying a hiking stick, why not make your own? Here's how to create your very own hiking stick for your next time on the trail.

1 Set out to find the perfect stick. A lot of times, this might be right in your own backyard or along a trail or sidewalk. Some places might have rules about not removing sticks from nature (like a state park or protected wildlife area), so if this is the case, find a new place to look for your perfect stick.

2 Examine your stick to really make sure it's a good one. Is it sturdy? Can you lean on it without it breaking? Is it the right height? You want to make sure that it's comfortable for you. Be sure to examine the overall size and how it feels when you hold it in your hand.

3 If your hiking stick needs some work, then do what you need to get it ready for the trail. This might include cutting (sawing) it down a bit if it's too tall. It could also include sanding it down so it doesn't give you splinters.

4 Every good hiking stick needs some personalization to really make it your own. Try wrapping the top of it in a comfortable material or even a decorative tape. Consider writing your name across it or adding beads or trinkets tied on it with string. This is your chance to put your own touch on your hiking stick.

5 Now it's time to hit the trails with your hiking stick. Take it on a short walk to start with. If that works out, go for a longer one each time. Be sure to use it to help you with those really steep climbs or as you're walking down a hill.

Jack's Top Tips and Takeaways

- **Find the right height.** Everybody has their height preference for the perfect hiking stick, but, generally speaking, here's a good rule: Stand with your arms at your sides. Your stick should be about 6 to 12 inches taller than your elbow.

- **Don't get distracted by a cool option.** Just because you find a really cool stick doesn't mean it's right for the job. If you find a supercool stick with a bunch of twists and turns, it probably won't make the best hiking option. Instead, find a strong, straight, and sturdy stick that you can decorate to make it unique.

22

FIND A HIKING TRAIL
TO GO BOULDERING.

IF YOU'VE THOUGHT ABOUT TRYING rock climbing, then bouldering is a good way to test it out. It's basically like climbing except you don't need special equipment or training. This is because the climbing is more horizontal than vertical. So you're usually hiking across rocks instead of up them. Some people refer to this as a "scramble."

1 Get the right equipment. While it is mostly true that you don't need special equipment like ropes and harnesses, you still want to have some bouldering essentials, like shoes with a good grip, clothing that will allow you to easily move around, and possibly even a hiking stick to help you go from one section of rocks to the next.

2 Now set your sights on finding a good spot for bouldering. You want to choose an area that you can really tackle and isn't too difficult. This can be a dangerous sport, leading to scrapes, twisted ankles, and falls, so you want your first bouldering attempt to be pretty low-key. Look for a place that has mostly flat terrain and good hiking trails with just some bouldering challenges built into it.

3 Practice in your backyard or neighborhood first. This might seem a little bit silly, but it really will get you ready and in shape for bouldering. Climb across logs, go over rocks, and work on being quick and nimble.

4 As you start out, go slowly. Even if you're hiking across small rocks, it's definitely tricky to go from one surface to the next. It requires a lot of balance and patience. Focus on conquering one section at a time.

5 As you build your confidence, pick up your speed slightly but not too much. This is how accidents happen. You will definitely pick up tips and tricks as you go, like knowing what's a stable surface, but speed should not be your first priority with bouldering.

Jack's Top Tips and Takeaways

- **Set up your own bouldering course.** You know how step 3 is to practice in your backyard? Set up an obstacle course—think Ninja Warrior! You can use chairs to jump over, logs to balance on, and even boxes to crawl through.

- **Adjust for the weather.** If it's damp or wet, the rocks will definitely be slippery. You might not like going extraslow, but you should. My mom knows this all too well. She broke her nose while going too fast on some rocks and logs.

- **Have quick reflexes.** Keep your hands out, slightly bent to your sides as you scramble; this way, if you take a fall, you're likely to catch yourself before you do any bodily damage.

23
CONQUER A 10-MILE HIKE.

NOW THAT YOU'VE DONE lots of hiking, it's time to set a tough goal. Then focus as you go out to achieve it. A 10-mile hike, especially in a single day, is no easy task. Make sure you're in shape.

1 Start your training. It might not seem like you need to train to do a 10-mile hike (it's just walking, right?), but this is definitely a mistake you don't want to make. Set up a training plan to slowly build up the number of miles you do so you can be ready on hiking day. *Outside* magazine has good hiking plans. Look for advice on their website, outsideonline.com.

2 Recruit a friend to join you. Not everyone likes to set goals as a team, but this is one situation where it's definitely a good idea. Having someone to train with and do the hike with will help you hold yourself accountable. This person can be a friend, a family member, or anyone who you can convince to hike 10 miles.

3 Tackle hills as part of your training. Many times, people will avoid hills completely because they are difficult or challenging. However, if you make them part of your regular training process, you will do much better on the day that you do your big hike. Hills naturally strengthen your legs and build endurance. Even though they're annoying, they're worth it.

4 Target your specific hiking area. You can do this step early on if you want. Some people might even want to put it as step 1 because they first find a cool hike they want to do, and then they start training for it. You definitely want to make sure you know and understand the hike you'll be doing, though. Knowing the specific terrain of the hike—like lots of hills or scrambles— helps you to tailor your training regime to that hike. The location should be factored into your training.

5 On your hiking day, be sure to pack lots of water. You do not want to run out on mile 7, so pack in more than you think you need to be sure. Plan for about 2 liters per person, but more always works, too. Also pack snacks that will give you energy, and get started on your hike early.

Jack's Top Tips and Takeaways

- **Go for the half.** If you really want to show off to your friends, add 3.1 miles to your hike to make it a half marathon. A 10-mile hike is quite the achievement on its own, but this is a good extra challenge.

- **Plan for 2 days.** A 10-mile hike is still very difficult. If you need to, plan to take a break or spend the night somewhere, and do the hike in 2 days instead. This is especially true if you're doing a really difficult hike. Camping overnight will allow you to catch your breath and get energy back in your body.

- **Go out early.** Almost no one likes to start early or get up before the sun, but in the long run, it's probably the best decision. This is especially true if it's going to be even a little bit hot during the day. It's always a good idea to hike in nice, cool conditions. Plan to stop and rest during peak heat times of the day.

≡ 24 ≡
GO ON A FULL-MOON HIKE.

IF YOU'VE NEVER HIKED BY THE LIGHT of the moon, then this is definitely something you'll want to check off your list. You might be surprised at how much light a full moon can give off on a clear and cloudless night. You shouldn't even need a flashlight.

1 Get a schedule of all the upcoming full moons. You can easily find this by doing a Google search. Many calendars will also list full moons. This will help you make a plan for when you can go.

2 Pack for a perfect full-moon hike experience. This is different for everyone. Do you want to hike a lot during the full moon? Pack plenty of snacks. Would you rather hang out and just watch it? Pack a blanket. Your experience is up to you. The only thing you should probably plan for sure is to hike with a friend as a safety precaution.

3 Check the weather before you go. Just because it's supposed to be a full moon doesn't mean it's going to be a clear and peaceful night. There might be rain, storms, or it could just be really cloudy. You don't want to get out there if there's not going to be a moon for you to see.

4 Make sure it's dark enough to enjoy the moon. This means you'll want to get away from the city lights. And you don't want to start hiking too early—going out about a half hour before sunset is a good plan. Part of enjoying the full moon is having it be as dark as possible.

5 Take the time to enjoy your hike. You can skip the pictures for this one. Chances are, they aren't going to turn out anyway because the moon is too far away. Really encourage yourself to unplug, put the electronics aside, and enjoy this cool nature experience with a friend.

Jack's Top Tips and Takeaways

- **Try a different day.** Hiking at night with a full moon is supercool, but hiking when it's almost a full moon works, too. If you see that the weather won't be great on the actual full moon, go the day before or day after. Chances are, you won't even know it's not a full moon.

- **Look for a local trip.** A lot of full-moon activities like paddle trips or just hiking are gaining popularity. Look for an experience like this and sign up for it. It might be part of a community event or experience, which can be really fun, and a great way to meet like-minded people.

25
GO SPELUNKING.

IF YOU DO A DICTIONARY SEARCH for spelunking, you'll see that it's defined as the exploration of caves. You might not think you have any caves near you to go spelunking in, but you probably do if you take a look. Even urban spelunking (exploring in cities or urban areas) is gaining in popularity, so put it on your list. Hiking underground is a whole new experience.

1 You want to find good spelunking opportunities in your area, and to do this, your first step is to do a basic Google search. By looking up spelunking, along with your city, state, or area, you'll probably find articles, websites, or discussions in forums about different areas where you can go. Seriously, there are probably places nearby that you've never even heard of.

2 Find a cave you really want to explore. Now keep in mind that you might need to travel a bit to have a good spelunking experience, but it'll definitely be worth it. If it's your first time, plan to go with a guide or as part of a tour. This is for safety reasons—you want to learn some basics from a pro.

3 Practice spelunking by hiking or exploring small spaces. This might include hiking between trees or crawling under your bed. This will get you used to maneuvering up, down, and all around to get to where you need to be.

4 Discover what equipment you might need. You might not need any if you're going to an area that has spelunking as an activity, which is a great way to try this hobby for the first time. In this case there are probably offer tours or experiences that you can sign up for. Then you won't need a thing.

5 Go underground. Now that you've trained and are prepared, go to your local cave and start exploring. Be sure to notice everything around you and compare how the underground looks different from aboveground. There are so many cool things to see and experience that you can't otherwise.

Jack's Top Tips and Takeaways

- **Look for a good headlamp.** Holding a flashlight in your hand when spelunking can be hard, so get a headlamp instead. Headlamps are much more effective because while climbing or moving around, you don't have to do anything except turn the power button on.

- **Conquer your fears.** Even if you are scared of the dark, you can still do this amazing activity. All you need are lights and equipment like a headlamp. If you have these things, it'll be like exploring a cave above the ground.

- **Know what you're getting into.** If you are claustrophobic, you might have an issue. Sometimes caves are only small spaces, which can be really scary to some. If this is the case, look for a big cave instead. Did you find one, but it's far away? Road trip!

26

HIKE IN THE GRAND CANYON.

THE HIKES IN THE GRAND CANYON are some of the most difficult and epic hikes you can do in the United States, and it's the toughest hiking challenge in this book. The good news, though, is that it's definitely possible. Thousands of people set out to hike in the Grand Canyon every year, so you can find tons of articles and tips to help you out and get you ready.

1 Find a time to go. Your first instinct might be to go in summer. This is possible, but it's probably not best because of the hot summer temps in the Southwest. However, winter isn't necessarily the answer either. It can get cold and even icy in the canyon during this time. Spring and fall are generally great times to hike in the Grand Canyon, but they have to work for your schedule, too. Do some planning on the best times to go, and try to go when the weather is not too hot. However, you'll always want to keep tourist season in mind (during school vacation weeks and holidays). This will lead to more crowded trails.

2 Choose the trail you want to go on. There are multiple ways to hike down into the Grand Canyon and then back up again. Some trails like the Bright Angel Trail are longer (but they're easier) while others like the South Kaibab Trail are shorter (but a lot more difficult). As a comparison, South Kaibab is 6.8 miles to the bottom and Bright Angel is 9.3. Some start on the north rim (which isn't as popular), while others start on the more popular south rim. Do the research to make sure you're choosing the right trail for you.

3 Make a plan of whether you're going to hike the whole thing in a day or if you're going to stay overnight in the canyon. If you do want to stay at the bottom, you better check into camping permits or lodging reservations. Both are limited, and you might have to plan up to months in advance. A huge word of warning is that it's very difficult to complete the Grand Canyon hike in a single day. Even trained, seasoned hikers don't do this. Plus, then you'll feel rushed instead of enjoying the experience. If you're going to camp or stay at the bottom for a night, plan ahead. You'll either need to make reservations or take gear with you.

4 Start as early in the day as possible. This is another very important step to consider. Most people don't like to get up super early, but if you're going to hike the entire canyon, you really need to. Not only will this allow you to beat the crowds, but it'll also help you get in a few miles before it gets to the hot (and uncomfortable) part of the day. Plan on taking at least 3 liters of water per person due to the heat and strenuous conditions.

5 Enjoy every second. The views are so amazing. Even if you've seen pictures of the Grand Canyon, there's nothing like seeing it for yourself. Take a few moments to just sit and take it all in. Be sure to take pictures along the way, too, because this is something you'll want to remember for many years to come. If you're looking for a quick pic of the canyon from the rim, there are numerous viewing stations featured throughout the national park.

Jack's Top Tips and Takeaways

- **Bring an extra pair of socks.** You will probably get dirty and sweaty on your trip up and down. So why socks? A clean, fresh pair of socks will make your tired, worn feet feel so much better. It might be just the thing to get you through.

- **Plan this hike as part of a special event.** This is a very cool, fun, but difficult trip. Think about planning to do this as part of a special event or accomplishment. I'm planning to hike in the Grand Canyon when I graduate high school. It's a good goal to have or something to dream about.

- **After you hike, raft!** If you have extra time to spare, check out the rafting trips through the Grand Canyon. This would be an amazing way to see a different side of the canyon.

TRAVELING

"NOT ALL THOSE WHO WANDER ARE LOST."

—J. R. R. TOLKIEN

Traveling is one of those hobbies that, once you start it, you won't ever want to stop. It doesn't matter if you stick close to home or visit faraway places; there's something really amazing about getting outside and just soaking up the natural beauty around you.

You can tackle this list from just about anywhere in the country. Most of the items don't have specific requirements of where you should go. You just need the willingness to explore and an open mind. Who knows where your adventures will take you!

27

VISIT AT LEAST FIVE NATIONAL PARKS.

WITH SIXTY NATIONAL PARKS in North America, there are plenty of options for you to choose from. If you want to keep it simple, choose the five national parks closest to you so you can drive to all of them. However, if you want more of a challenge, pick national parks all over the country so you really have to go near and far to hit them all.

1 Learn more about the national parks and where they are. Start your search at nps.gov/findapark. You can search by state to see all the national parks or national monuments within each one. Another good website for starting your search is parktrust.org, which includes a great interactive map to help you research the parks.

2 Discover unique experiences or adventures you want to have at the national parks. For instance, are you into whitewater rafting? Glacier and the Grand Canyon are both great national parks for this. Want to see whales? Try Acadia National Park. Looking for classic or monumental experiences? Seeing Old Faithful in Yellowstone or climbing in Yosemite are both popular adventures.

3 Make a top 10 list of national parks you want to visit. As you read about the different parks, you'll likely want to visit much more than five or ten, so it helps to have a short list of "must visit" parks you'd like to get to. If you have big dreams, like going to national parks in Hawaii or Alaska, then you might want to include a few options that are easier to get to as well.

4 Make a plan before you go. Many national parks are popular and busy. For the best experience, plan your trip for when you know it's a good time to visit (so look at weather for the

area). And have an idea of the top things you want to do in each park. For instance, most parks will have many hiking trails, but others might specialize in climbing or paddling (for example), so knowing what you want to accomplish in each park ahead of time helps you plan your trip.

5 Write down your adventures. Go out and enjoy the public land during the day, but then at night, take a moment to write down your favorite parts of the park and what you did. If you can capture these memories while they're still fresh, this is best. It might seem like a small thing, but you will love reading it one day.

Jack's Top Tips and Takeaways

- **Wake up early.** I love to sleep in and get my sleep, but sometimes I wake up early to avoid crowds at national parks. You may just find the best experiences are those without the crowds.

- **The visitor center is where you will learn the best places to go and all of the information.** The park rangers in the visitor center always want to help give you the best spots and all of the cool information. You can also find good places to go in nearby areas.

- **It's hard to see an entire national park in 1 or 2 days.** You should always give yourself an extra day or two just in case you need more time to explore.

28
SPEND AN ENTIRE DAY
SEARCHING FOR WATERFALLS.

BIG OR SMALL, WATERFALLS IN NATURE never seem
to disappoint. Even the little ones seem to bring on calm and
relaxation. There's just something soothing about the flowing of
water, hidden among the hiking trails. Plus, the best part of all is
the hunt and anticipation in finding one. How many waterfalls
can you find in a single day?

1 Pick a good time of year. Spring is often the best time to go on a waterfall hunt because spring showers and the thawing of winter ice and snow maximizes the water in the area, but any time of the year can be good for waterfalls, if you know where to go. The last thing you want to do is go on an epic waterfall hunt only to find out that most of them are all dried up.

2 Ask the locals for their advice. Whether you're close at home or on a trip, it'll pay off to ask the workers at your local park or nature center about the waterfalls in the area. They might even know about hidden or little-known falls that aren't on a map. They'll also know what kind of condition they are in at the moment so you know if it's worth it to make the hike.

3 Make a map of your waterfall route, and set a goal. If you're going to a single location and planning to hike to all of them, this will help you stick to a plan. Or if you're driving to different locations to see the waterfalls, a map will help you figure out the best route to take so you can hit up as many as possible.

4 Hit the trails! Most waterfalls are going to be a little bit off the beaten path. So now it's time to hit the trails for a good day of hiking. You'll want to wear good shoes and pack plenty of water and snacks. If you have a really lofty goal in mind, then you'll have to keep moving.

5 Document every single waterfall with a photo. It'll help you remember the memory later on, and then you could even start your own photo collage of all the waterfalls you visit. This is a great way to decorate the front of your fridge or a bulletin board in your room.

Jack's Top Tips and Takeaways

- A nearby nature center might be a great place to find waterfalls to hike to. Nature center workers love to share good spots to find beautiful and unique waterfalls in the area.

- Bring a swimsuit along. At some waterfalls it's possible to swim at the bottom or get really close to the waterfall. Go ahead, be adventurous!

- Not all of the tallest waterfalls are the best. Sometimes there are smaller waterfalls that are just as beautiful, or even prettier, than taller ones. Some smaller waterfalls might create rainbows or be surrounded by smooth river rocks. Taller waterfalls, while majestic in their own right, may not have as many unique, detailed features.

= 29 =
PLAN A ROAD TRIP INTO NATURE.

ALL ROAD TRIPS ARE A GOOD IDEA, but those that take you to beautiful places in nature are even better. This is your chance to discover a hidden gem in your state or explore your region in a whole new way. Definitely plan to go off the beaten path a bit, because you never know what you will find.

1 Pick a location. Now, you shouldn't necessarily feel like you have to come up with a perfect plan to follow exactly. But having a general destination is a good idea. Start by looking up great nature destinations within 5 hours of your home. Look in every direction possible, and then narrow down your choices.

2 For your top two or three destinations, map out all the good stops along the way. This is definitely worth taking the time to do. Roadtrippers and Waze are two apps that can help you find cool things to see along your route. Looking up fun stops or roadside adventures to have on your way to your destination will make the trip a lot more fun. At a minimum, look up parks, nature centers, and wildlife areas or protected lands that you'll come across on your way. They're worth a pit stop!

3 Pack the perfect road trip supplies. Every good road trip should have great snacks, good books, and great entertainment. Put together a cooler of your favorite treats, which will definitely save you money as you make stops along your route. Also pack a good book, and plan for entertainment. You can play car games (20 Questions, Never Have I Ever, and

Would You Rather). Or look for family-friendly podcasts or an audio book everyone can listen to.

4 Hit the road. Start out early if you can because this will leave more time for fun stops along the way. This is an important part of the experience . . . taking time to explore as you go. You don't want to be so focused on your destination that you miss cool sights, activities, and adventures.

5 Don't be afraid to take a detour. Every good road trip needs to have some unknown to it—or at least some flexibility to make it up as you go. If you are traveling on highways or interstates, don't be afraid to exit and check out a small town off the beaten path. These are often great places to find hidden nature treasures.

Jack's Top Tips and Takeaways

- **Sometimes long road trips can get boring.** So, you could just play some games like Flip, or I Spy, or even 20 Questions. Or you could play an automated game like The Game of Life.

- **Try impromptu car games, too.** Guess-the-song games are fun, impromptu games for the car. Have one person pick songs and the other people guess the songs.

- **A road trip is a great excuse to bring a tent or a hammock.** You might not make it to your final destination on the first day, so try to make it as far as possible and then just use that tent or hammock for an overnight snooze.

30
VISIT EVERY PARK WITHIN 10 MILES OF YOUR HOME.

DID YOU KNOW THERE ARE PROBABLY PARKS in your own city and neighborhood that you've never heard of or been to? It's true! This challenge will really encourage you to get to know your area better. Or, if you're the type that goes to the same place or park over and over again, it'll encourage you to branch out a bit.

1 Find every park within 10 miles of your home. You might think you already know about the parks around your house, but this is the time to dig deep. You'll want to locate every tiny neighborhood park and destination to complete this challenge. Use Google maps to punch in your address and do a search. There have to be at least a few that you've never been to. If you live in a really small town or one that doesn't have a lot of parks, take this challenge to a more urban area. It's a great way to explore a new area.

2 Now that you know the parks in your area, create a map of every park you want to visit. You can do this by printing out a map online and then making little markers. Or you can draw your entire map by hand. Be sure to note each park's name and address.

3 Set a goal to complete this challenge by a certain day and time. This will depend on how many parks you have on your list. If you have twenty-plus parks, maybe this is a summer goal that you work on over several weeks. If you don't have that many parks on the list, try to complete this challenge in just a week or two.

4 Really take time to experience each park. Most will have playgrounds you can check out, but what else can you do at each park? Perhaps you take chalk to one and write fun messages and kind phrases for others to enjoy. Or maybe you plan a picnic lunch or to meet up with friends. Try to treat this challenge as an adventure and do something at each park to make it memorable.

5 Share your park adventures with others. It's great if you want to bring along a friend to some of your destinations, but another way to do this is to just tell others about great places in your area. Reminding people that there are amazing parks and public lands to enjoy is a wonderful service to your community.

Jack's Top Tips and Takeaways

- **Up the challenge by doing multiple park visits in a day.** Grab a buddy and see how many parks you can visit in a day. A variation on this is to challenge your buddy to see who can visit the most parks in that day— the winner gets a prize of his choice.

- **Going slow and steady can still make it fun.** Allow yourself to linger, and surprise yourself with your itinerary. Put all the parks in a hat and draw the name of which one you will go to next.

- **Be flexible.** If you need more parks to visit or if there's too many to visit in 1 day, just change the radius of your park search around your house. You can change it to 5 miles or 30 miles as long as you are having fun and exploring new things.

31
WATCH THE SUNRISE AND SUNSET IN A SINGLE DAY.

WAKING UP TO A GORGEOUS SUNRISE is a beautiful way to start the day. And seeing the sun set is a wonderful way to end the day. So why not combine the two to have a truly epic experience? To make the most of this challenge, you just need great places for viewing.

1 Find your destination to watch the sunrise. The best place to catch a sunrise is usually from a high point. This will allow you to get a good view as the sun slowly rises up above the skyline. Of course, you'll also want this place to be facing the east because the sun rises in the east and sets in the west. If you're at home, look for high points or towers you could climb to catch the sunrise. If you're traveling, ask the locals where good spots are for sunrise.

2 Find your destination to watch the sunset. For the sunset, you'll want a wide-open viewpoint. This is because, as the sun goes down in the west, it's easy for buildings, trees, or hills to block your view. Another high point can be a great spot for sunset. Open water is also a good, classic option.

3 On the day of your challenge, get up early. You can usually google "When is sunrise?" and, based on your location, you'll get the answer right there. However, you want to get set before that time. If sunrise is at 6:12, for instance, try to be in place at least 30 minutes beforehand. This is such a great experience to really see how the day wakes up with the sun.

4 Get ready for sunset at least an hour before the expected time. Again, you can do a Google search about sunset for the area and get a general time. And this time you'll want to be in place about an hour beforehand. Take a blanket, bring along a game, or make a sweet treat to have. You'll love watching the show in the sky as the night creeps in all around you.

5 Now that you've seen the sunrise and sunset in the same day, repeat this experience. Travel somewhere cool, or challenge yourself to do this while on vacation. It takes a little extra effort (especially the waking up early part), but it's totally worth it.

Jack's Top Tips and Takeaways

- **By the shoreline of a body of water is a great place to see the sunrise and sunset.** Going near a body of water when the sun rises and sets offers you a clear view of the beautiful imagery in the sky. The reflection from the sun to the water is also really beautiful.

- **Bring gear to keep you warm.** Early in the morning and later at night can be a little chilly, so bring along blankets or a jacket to ensure you're warm enough to hang around long enough for the shows.

32

GO STARGAZING IN THE MIDDLE OF NOWHERE.

STARGAZING IS ALWAYS A GOOD WAY to get outside and experience the great outdoors, but it's particularly awesome when you go somewhere amazing to do it. The best way to see the stars is to go to a remote, empty area where there's no city light for miles and miles. This experience will completely change the way you view the night sky.

1 Pick a destination. You could pick a place near your home, but we recommend using this as an excuse to travel. Think of a place that you've always wanted to go to, and then look for a remote area out in nature that you can travel to. This will be the perfect place to go gazing for stars.

2 Study up on your stars. Learning your constellations is such a rewarding experience. Once you teach yourself how to pick out some of the basic constellations, like the Big Dipper, Little Dipper, Taurus, and Orion, you'll always be able to find them in the night sky. Keep in mind that winter and summer constellations can be different, so know what you're looking for at the right time of year.

3 Set a goal of the constellations you want to see during your stargazing. This should be based on your research of time of year and not just constellations you find interesting. Don't just pick all easy ones. Challenge yourself to find some of the unusual or hard-to-spot ones, as well.

4 Pack your bags for a night of gazing. Some of the items you might want to bring along include a flashlight, a blanket, a star map guide, snacks, a pillow, and some extra clothes to keep you warm.

5 Get to your location early so you can scope out a good spot. You can even bring along a picnic dinner and watch the sunset as it gets dark enough for stargazing. One of the most magical experiences is actually watching the stars appear in the sky, one by one. It's like you can see the constellations forming right before your eyes.

Jack's Top Tips and Takeaways

- **Bring bug spray along.** Not a lot of people like being bitten by mosquitoes. That's why you should bring bug spray along, to avoid that mess.

- **Check the weather on the night you will go.** You don't want clouds in the forecast because then you won't see all the stars. If it's rainy or super cold, you don't want to stargaze in those elements. Since weather isn't always predictable, be flexible in your plans to stargaze.

- **Look up different constellations.** Stargazing in the middle of nowhere is awesome on its own, but if you and your family or friends can spot different, rarer constellations, that is epic.

33
VISIT A HOT SPRINGS.

HOT SPRINGS ARE SOME OF THE COOLEST, puzzling, and awesome natural wonders of nature. They seem to pop up out of nowhere, and then it's like having your very own hot tub in the great outdoors. You might have to travel a bit to find real hot springs because they don't just show up anywhere. They're worth the trip, though. It's like a really beautiful natural swimming hole—hot springs are just a part of nature that you have to experience for yourself.

1 Learn more about hot springs, particularly the ones that are perfectly fine to swim in and those that aren't. Believe it or not, not all hot springs are approved for humans. The term "hot springs" might be the more general term that people use, but these bodies of water are actually thermal. If you want to learn more about this type of natural energy, visit americangeosciences.org. The way that a lot of hot springs (but not all) are heated is related to volcanic energy. Wikipedia has a pretty great description about hot springs.

2 Discover where the best hot springs are. Here's where you'll want to head to americangeosciences.org again. They have a really cool map you can check out to see all hot springs throughout the country. Spoiler alert: Most are in the West!

3 Make a hot springs top 5 list. As you click on the map, start making a list of interesting hot springs that you'd like to visit. Pick places that wow you and make you want to travel to see them. If you don't live near hot springs, then you're going to have to travel anyway. So you might as well make the trip worthwhile.

4 Pack for your day of soaking and adventuring. You will likely need a bathing suit, sandals, towels, sunscreen, snacks, and lots of water to stay hydrated. Most of the hot springs throughout North America are not fancy at all. They're a lot like going swimming at a local lake or pond, so be sure to bring along everything that you need for the whole day.

5 Take it all in—the sights, sounds, and smells! This is truly a nature experience that a lot of people will never get to have. You want to remember every single minute of it. Take pictures. Notice the natural beauty. And soak it all in (both literally and with your eyes).

Jack's Top Tips and Takeaways

- **It's supercool and fun to go in the winter.** Hot springs will always be hot year-round. A winter escape to a hot springs is much like a dip in a hot tub at a resort. Don't forget your towels and blankets for when you get out.

- **Hot springs can smell like sulfur.** Many hot springs give off a sulfuric "rotten egg" odor, but the experience will be worth it despite that smell. It is part of nature. Also, your nose stops smelling familiar smells after a while—this is called olfactory fatigue.

34

SEE THE NORTHERN LIGHTS.

THE NORTHERN LIGHTS SEEM LIKE this magical phenomenon that you can only see in movies or fairy tales, but they are actually pretty easy to see. You just have to know where to go, and then go during the right time of year. This is probably the most challenging task in this chapter because most people don't live near the northern lights. But this one will definitely amaze you.

1 Learn what the northern lights are. There's a fantastic description on this website, northernlightscentre.ca. Basically, it tells you that the northern lights are these bright and colorful lights that show up in the sky because of electrically charged particles from the sun. You can see them in both the Northern and Southern Hemispheres. So in North America, your best chance of seeing them is in Alaska or Canada. During certain times of the year, the visibility can dip down into the United States a bit, but this isn't that common.

2 Learn when the best time of year is to see the northern lights. For the United States, this will be winter. Why is this? It's because winter is made up of long, dark nights. So there are longer, darker periods of time in which you can see them.

3 Plan a trip to a northern lights area. If you're lucky enough to live near the northern lights, then this one will be easy for you. But for the rest of us, it'll likely take a trip to the right place and during the right time of year. Don't expect to go to a place and see the northern lights in a single night. Instead, plan a trip where you'll be there for several days. This will greatly increase your chance of seeing them.

4 Check the weather, and check the northern lights forecast. You can also look up an aurora forecast online to increase your chances.

5 Get out there and have your northern lights adventure. Much like going to see the stars, you want to go to the middle of nowhere for the best view. You don't want any city lights interrupting your experience. You will want to take a camera because with a little practice, you can get amazing pictures.

Jack's Top Tips and Takeaways

- **The northern lights are beautiful so make it last.** Bring a camera or video to record the experience so you can see the northern lights forever.

- **Make sure to be prepared.** Be prepared by bringing cameras, food, water, and all other supplies.

- **Find the best spot to see the northern lights.** Some spots are better than others to see the northern lights. Research the best places to go, like areas with limited ground light.

BIKING

"LIFE IS LIKE RIDING A BICYCLE. IN ORDER TO KEEP YOUR BALANCE, YOU MUST KEEP MOVING."

—ALBERT EINSTEIN

You can explore so many great places with just two wheels. Bicycles are such an important part of childhood. From the little trikes when you're a toddler to the much bigger bikes with gears and fancy tires, they are a great way to explore nature. Plus, there are a lot of great benefits to them.

You get great exercise every time you ride. Bikes allow you to get closer to fields, streams, and other parts of nature that you can't get to on just a road. And they're fun! The challenges in this chapter will truly push you to your limits and encourage you to get the most out of your bike. There's even an epic 100-mile challenge to conquer. Time to get pedaling!

35
BIKE TO A PICNIC LUNCH.

YOU CAN BE PRETTY MUCH ANYWHERE to check this one off your list. Whether you're at home or on vacation somewhere, this is a good challenge. Try to push yourself to go somewhere that's not just around the corner or in the neighborhood. It'll make you appreciate your experience that much more!

1 Get your bike ready. Whether you're going 3 miles or 23 miles, you need to make sure your bike is fully tuned up. Check the air in the tires. Make sure the pedals move smoothly and there are no issues. You don't want to get halfway into a ride and then have something go wrong.

2 Gather the right accessories for biking to a picnic. It's not easy to carry an entire lunch or dinner along on a bike, so you need to plan accordingly. If you have a bike basket or platform where you can attach a bag, you should be all set. If not, you should be able to wear a backpack just fine.

3 Make a good lunch for a picnic, but also one that can fit the limited space on your bike (or in your backpack). Stick with items that aren't heavy, and try to minimize the number of sides or drinks you bring along. It's best if you can figure out exactly how much lunch you need so when you're finished, you can gain back space (and weight).

4 Set a destination and go. Local parks make great picnic destinations. They often have picnic tables already set up, so you won't have to bring along a blanket to sit on. Plus, they'll have a playground, bike trails, or other activities to check out after you eat.

5 Once you're done with lunch, take time to check out the area around your picnic area and enjoy some relaxing time before you head back.

Jack's Top Tips and Takeaways

- **Bring water packets for extra flavor.** Sometimes you get tired of just water. To save space, bring flavored water packets that can be added to your standard drinking water. The packets will help you save weight but still allow you to have the tasty flavors found in sports drinks.

- **Install bottle holders on your bike to save space.** If you install bottle holders, you don't have to carry something heavy in your backpack.

36
LEARN HOW TO
CHANGE A BIKE TIRE.

IF YOU'RE GOING TO RIDE A BIKE AT ALL, then you should know how to change its tire. You never know when something might happen and you suddenly pop a tire out of nowhere. Or your tire just slowly wears down, and then you need to replace it. By learning how to do it yourself, you'll save time and money. Plus, if you're in an emergency situation, you'll be OK!

1 Remove the tire. If you're unsure of how to do this, check out a video on YouTube (there are plenty). It helps if you have your bike propped up or even upside down for this. Then you'll be able to get a close look after you pull it off the frame of your bike.

2 Find the problem in the tire. Check for a tear or hole in the inner tube because you might be able to repair it. Carefully and slowly run your fingers along the inside of the tire. The item that made the tire flat could still be there, and it's probably sharp. If you do find the item, make sure you remove it completely.

3 Either repair the current inner tube, or purchase an inner tube for the bike. If it's just a small tear, you'll likely be able to fix it with a spray-on product. (Search "fix a flat bike tire" on Amazon or online, and you'll see several options.) Mount the inner tube inside the tire and put the tire back on the rim, making sure it's secure all the way around.

4 Pump up the new tire. This is where you'll check your seal to make sure you have the new tire on correctly. If you don't, take it off and try again. Put the wheel back on your bike. Check that it's secure in the frame.

5 Give it a test ride. You'll want to go slowly at first to make sure everything is secure and in place. If it does OK with a little bit of weight, try a longer distance. Make sure the tire will hold up before you take your bike on another long ride.

Jack's Top Tips and Takeaways

- **Carry a repair kit.** You will love having a kit with you to fix a flat tire whenever you are riding. You can buy these kinds of kits on Amazon or at a bike store. Having one of these kits with you means you will likely always be able to fix a flat tire yourself.

- **Check your whole bike thoroughly.** While you're on tire repair, it's a good idea to check the rest of your bike to see if there are any other things that you need to fix.

37

BIKE TO A FARMERS' MARKET.

WHY BIKE TO A FARMERS' MARKET? It's such a great summer spot, and you can find one in most cities and neighborhoods. Plus these markets tend to be very bike-friendly (and car parking may be limited anyway). Here's how you can have a truly cool experience biking to—and enjoying—the farmers' market.

1 Bring a backpack to use for your shopping. Now find the closest farmers' market. If you live in a city, you'll likely have many to choose from that are open on multiple days. Or if you live in a smaller town, you may be limited to finding open markets on weekends, specific days of the week, or sometimes even certain seasons.

2 Have breakfast or lunch at the market. So many farmers' markets have food trucks or stands that you can eat at. Plan to make this a real experience and spend some time at the market. One of the best ways to do this is by sampling some local food or flavor.

3 After you've had a bite to eat, take time to walk around the market and enjoy the experience. Talk to the farmers or local artists, and ask them about what they have. Most are really friendly, and they love telling you about themselves. It's a good way to get to know the local community. Buy something fresh or homemade to take home (thus, the backpack).

4 Pack up your goods and hit the road. It can be so tempting to spend lots of money at a farmers' market, but pick your favorite one or two items, and then head home. Be careful not to overload your backpack, as you want it to be centered on your body and not be so heavy that it might cause you to lose your balance and fall.

5 Use your farmers' market excursion as a jumping-off point to bike to other locations. Plan your next biking adventure in the neighborhood. Perhaps you'll bike to a nearby park to play basketball. Or maybe you'll make a trip to the library. There are so many great community and neighborhood destinations you can reach by bicycle. When the weather is good, it makes for such a nice day.

Jack's Top Tips and Takeaways

- **Make sure your bike is secure so it won't get stolen.** Bring a lock when you go to keep your bike secure. Really good locks can be expensive, but they are worth it.

- **Think outside the box on places to go.** Don't just go to a farmers' market. Maybe you want to go to a nearby store, too. My personal favorite place to go is a smoothie stand. Look for a bikeable place near you that you want to check out.

- **Convince your whole family to go somewhere.** For an even more memorable experience, convince your family to bike somewhere together. You get to share in the experience while also helping the environment because you won't be going in a car. That's a win-win!

38

TRY MOUNTAIN BIKING.

MOUNTAIN BIKING IS NOT LIKE RIDING a regular bicycle. It's a challenging, bumpy ride. As a result, this is a sport that you'll want to ease into a little at a time. Start off with a short ride with someone who knows what they're doing, and then grow from there. Oh, and you might want to consider investing in a pair of padded bike shorts—it'll minimize some of the aches the next day.

1 Use the right type of bike. Mountain bikes have thicker, stronger tires than regular bikes. Think of it like having hiking shoes instead of regular shoes. If you don't have a bike with strong tires, you do not want to take it out on the trail. The tires just won't hold up. If you don't have a mountain bike, consider borrowing or renting one instead.

2 Go to a good spot for mountain biking. Just do a Google search for "mountain biking" in your area, or pick up a local guidebook, and you'll quickly find places to go. You might even find places where you can rent equipment if you want to try out the sport for the first time. Look for a trail that is good for beginners, and avoid anything that says "expert" or "strenuous."

3 Watch your speed. Go slowly until you get the hang of it. You might be tempted to just take off and go fast, but this is not a good idea. Some of the trail you'll go over will be uneven ground, often with root systems protruding. Most of the trails aren't paved, so you need to get used to those bumps along the way.

4 Be cautious as you tackle the hills. Like with road cycling, you won't ever truly be sitting on an incline or a downhill. You'll want to lean forward a little bit as you go up hills, and lean back a bit as you go down. Meanwhile, your knees should be strong but not locked into place so you can bounce along with the bumps on the trail or track.

5 Watch where you're going at all times. This is so important with mountain biking because riding over even one hole can cause a major accident. When you first get started, stick to flat, secure ground. As you gain knowledge and confidence, you can try going over small sticks and rocks. But you should not attempt this until you're ready!

Jack's Top Tips and Takeaways

- **Safety comes first.** Always think about safety when you are mountain biking. I always wear a helmet when mountain biking and you should as well. Mountain biking is dangerous because of the hazards on the trail—rocks, branches, tree roots, fallen trees, and much more. By wearing a helmet, you prevent these hazards from damaging your head. And, for the record, you should wear a helmet when you're regular biking, too.

- **Don't be afraid to ask for help.** If you know someone who is really good at mountain biking, you should have him take you along on one of his familiar trails. He could give you tips on maneuvering around hazards and offer ways to increase the fun level while out on the trail.

39
COMPLETE A CENTURY RIDE.

ARE YOU READY FOR A CHALLENGE? A century ride is 100 miles. This might sound really intimidating at first, but with the right training (and a bit of determination), you'll easily be able to tackle it.

1 Look for a century ride near you. If this is your first one and you're not used to biking much, then it might be best to look for an organized ride to join. Century rides are a lot like marathons or triathlons. They are held all over the country for cyclists. So find one near you, and put it on your calendar. This will be a good way to set a goal and date. It also means built-in water stops along the way via the ride organizers, and they'll also be on the lookout for safety issues.

2 Train for your ride. If you're looking for a good training plan, go to bicycling.com and search for "century ride training plan." There's an 8-week program that you can do, but if you're new to cycling, opt for a 4- to 6-month training program instead. You'll want to have the right equipment and hydration for training. Bike shorts can really make a difference with the aches and pains that come with a long ride, and it's always good to have plenty of water.

3 Recruit a friend to help you train to hold yourself accountable. Maybe you're the type to always be accountable and stick to your goal. If so, this is awesome. If not, then a biking buddy will help you hold to your training schedule. When training, don't

look too far out in front. Look to accomplish one week's goals first before moving on to the next week. Write down your goals on a calendar so you can check them off as you meet them.

4 Work up to your long rides. As with many training plans, there will be a day where you do a long ride each week. Sometimes you're biking for a few hours at a time. Really challenge yourself on these days by working hard on the uphills and trying to increase your speed during part of the ride. This training will pay off.

5 Tackle your ride. Have a good dinner the night before ride day. Then get up early, have a light breakfast, and drink plenty of water. Know the route you will take, even if it will be marked for you if you're part of a group or ride challenge. Have an idea of the stops you want to make along the way to take a break or get some more water. No matter how you ride, even if there are plenty of people passing you, go at your own pace.

Jack's Top Tips and Takeaways

- **Participate in training around your area.** If there is a good group training program for a century ride, you should sign up immediately. Also, look for someone who might also be doing a century ride to train with that person. Find someone who is at about your pace or maybe even a bit faster to challenge you to keep up.

- **Be respectful if you are riding with people.** There is a lot of etiquette involved in ride events. One thing you can do is to learn how to signal when you are turning. This way no one gets hurt . . . or angry.

- **Make sure you have the best bike for the ride.** It could be unwise if you use a mountain bike for a century ride, where road bikes with thinner wheels are more ideal. Learn the right kind of bike and equipment you'll need and get it.

WILDLIFE
WATCHING

"THE IDEA OF WILDERNESS NEEDS NO DEFENSE, IT ONLY NEEDS DEFENDERS."

—EDWARD ABBEY

From birds in the sky to whales in the sea, there are so many great opportunities to see wildlife around the world. There's something truly special about watching animals in their natural habitats. It makes you realize just how big this world is and how humans are only part of it.

Of course, you should always keep your distance when watching wildlife. Remember they are wild animals and the wildland is their home. If you can remember this and help do your part to protect the land around the world, then it will help protect wildlife for many years to come.

⋹ 40 ⋸
GO BIRD WATCHING.

BIRD WATCHING IS A HUGE HOBBY. Millions of people feed birds in their backyards every year so they can get a closer look at them. Plus many others go out to beautiful, majestic places just so they can see rare and unique birds. Whether you want to stay in your backyard or go out in nature, bird watching is a great way to see wildlife.

1 Learn the birds in your backyard. This is the first step in watching birds. See what birds you notice in your own backyard, and learn about them. You might want to identify them so you know what you're looking at. Our favorite bird book to recommend is the *Kaufman Field Guide*. It does a good job of explaining the basics and telling you what to look for.

2 Learn about the birds in your area. Definitely expand your bird watching beyond your backyard. There actually is only a small population of birds that will even go into backyards to nest or for food. So there's a whole other world of birds to look for in your area. They can be so beautiful and colorful, too. Look for a bird book (or pick up a brochure at a local nature center) that focuses on birds specifically in your area or state so that you can really hone in on learning about your local popuations.

3 Borrow a good set of binoculars. Binoculars, especially good ones, make bird watching such a great experience. You can often borrow a basic set at a nature center. One of the top qualities to look for is that they are easy to adjust (focus) on the top. Having a good set of binoculars will make seeing the birds so much clearer.

4 Look for a bird walk to join. Many nature centers or Audubon locations have free, guided bird walks, which are particularly good for you to join if you are new to bird watching. Spring and

fall are both popular times for bird walks, but spring is especially awesome as birds are migrating north and getting ready for nesting season. Those who lead bird walks are so excited to welcome new birders, so don't be intimidated to just show up. They will help you see so many more bird species than you would on your own.

5 Now that you know the basic characteristics of some birds in your area, keep an eye out for signs of them. Look for nests, holes in trees, and even bird poop to help you locate birds. You can often see a lot just by paying attention out on a hike or walk. Also when you're out, listen for their songs. Just being aware of bird signs around you will help you see more.

Jack's Top Tips and Takeaways

- **Ask someone for help if you need it.** If you can't get the hang of binoculars right away, don't be afraid to ask someone. You'll find other birders who would love to help.

- **Go to different habitats for different birds.** If you want to see certain birds, it helps to know their habitat. For instance, near the water you'll find a lot of geese, ducks, cranes, and herons. If you want to see roadrunners, you have to go to the desert or the Southwest. If you want to see a hummingbird, try a garden with lots of flowers.

= 41 =
FIND A BALD EAGLE'S NEST.

BALD EAGLES HAVE UNIQUE nest-building habits because they will use the same nest year after year. They just keep adding to it, and eventually, that nest can weigh more than 2 tons! This means once you find a bald eagle's nest, you can probably look forward to seeing it for many years. But first you have to find it.

1 Know what you're looking for. Do a Google search for an eagle's nest, and you'll see that it's a giant pile of sticks usually in the high top of a tree.

2 Now look high . . . very, very high. Once you know what you're looking for, you need to know where to look. Eagles like to build their nest, made up of a group of sticks, in forested areas, and at the very top of trees. This may mean that you have to break out a pair of binoculars. Eagles are early nesters, meaning they start their nesting in very early spring. This is good news if you're trying to find an eagle's nest because the leaves on the trees haven't budded out yet. This makes it easier to find a grouping of sticks.

3 Ask around to birders in the area. Chances are that local birders will know where to find an eagle's nest. Go to a bird group or a nature center, and tell them that you really want to see an eagle's nest. Ask them if they would be willing to share information about where to find one in your area.

4 Once you find one, observe from a distance. All bird nests are protected by law, so this means you cannot get close to

one, touch the eggs, or interfere with the nesting process. It's important to only watch from a distance and with binoculars. Be respectful, and don't get too close.

5 Now challenge yourself to find an owl's nest or a hummingbird's nest. If you conquered an eagle's nest, move on to an owl's nest. They like to keep their nests hidden, and they're very tough to find. Or look for a hummingbird's nest, which is very tiny. Both will be a good challenge.

Jack's Top Tips and Takeaways

- **Eagles' nests can be hard to find.** You'll have a better chance of finding one by bringing binoculars along. Use these to look for big masses of sticks and leaves way up in a tree.

- **Look for a *big* nest.** It isn't just a robin's nest or a small gathering of twigs. It's also a lot bigger than a squirrel's nest. Look for a big gathering of sticks several feet across.

- **If you see an eagle, follow it.** If you see an eagle, you might try following it to see where it goes. You might be able to follow it to its nest.

42
IDENTIFY ANIMAL TRACKS.

FINDING ANIMAL TRACKS WHEN you're outside is really exciting. It's fun to think that there was a wild animal passing through days, hours, or even minutes before you. Naturally, you want to know who the tracks belong to, and with a little practice, you can. This challenge will help you gain the skills to recognize and identify animal tracks in the wild.

1 Get a good tracks book or find an online resource. This will make a huge difference as you learn about animal tracks for the first time because this is such a visual challenge. Look at and study different animal tracks, and make note of size (both length and width) and overall shape. You can use your own hand as a comparison.

2 Study and learn the most common animal tracks. If you do a Google search of "most common animal tracks," you'll get several results and posters. It will depend on where you live, but the most common tracks you'll likely see in the wild include raccoon, rabbit, deer, weasel, turkey, fox, and coyote. Identify the differences among those tracks. For example, there's a huge difference in deer tracks (which are hooves) versus fox (which can look like cat or dog paws). By learning the most common tracks, you'll be able to quickly narrow down what you're looking at when you're out in the wild.

3 In addition to tracks, you can find other clues to help you narrow in on what kind of animal was in the area. One of the best ways to do this is by looking for animal poop (aka scat). The size and shape of this can vary a lot from one animal to the next, so if you find tracks, look for poop nearby. Yes, there are also charts, graphs, posters, and even entire books about animal scat.

4 Put your skills into practice. Once you've learned some basic information about animal tracks, it's time to go outside and find some tracks so you can identify them. The best time to look for animal tracks is when the ground is softer, so a day after a rain can be perfect. Another tip is to look around ponds, rivers, and other areas of water. This is because they are usually muddy or softer areas where there's an opportunity for the animals to make a good indent or impression in the ground. If you can, take your

book with you to help you figure out the track "in the field." If not, take a picture, and then study it at home.

5 Now challenge a family member or friend to an animal-tracking challenge. Make printouts of animal tracks (without the name) and place them throughout your backyard to identify. Or go out into the wild to see how many tracks you can find and identify in an hour. This would be a good team challenge, too.

Jack's Top Tips and Takeaways

- Be sure to pay attention to every detail in the tracks. This is because the length of a certain claw or the distance between each claw might help you determine which animal made it.

- You can also look for tracks that don't have feet. For example, you can find snake tracks in the dirt or mud. Snakes might not have legs, but they still leave tracks for you to find.

- Challenge yourself to find the differences in similar tracks. For example, dog tracks and coyote tracks are very similar, so look closely. Even though the differences between coyote tracks and dog tracks are very difficult to see, it would be a good challenge to tackle.

43

SEARCH FOR A MONARCH, A CATERPILLAR, AND THE EGGS.

MONARCHS ARE THE MOST POPULAR butterfly in America. Many people recognize them easily because they are bright orange and black. They've also gotten a lot of attention in recent years because their numbers are declining. They need milkweed (a plant) to live, so a lot people try to encourage others to plant more of this native plant. Plus, milkweed is the key to your success in being able to find a monarch, a caterpillar, and the eggs.

1 Find a monarch. This one will probably be pretty easy because monarchs are big and brightly colored. Just about any garden or nature area with plants is an appealing place for monarchs to hang out. They fly from flower to flower, looking for nectar.

2 Now learn what milkweed looks like. You can find monarch butterflies without knowing what milkweed is, but you won't be able to do this for the caterpillar or eggs. This is because the monarch butterfly only lays her eggs on milkweed plants. Then the caterpillars only eat milkweed. Do a Google search for "common milkweed" or "swamp milkweed" so you know what it looks like. The plant tends to have pink flowers, and it's common in wild areas or fields where wildflowers grow.

3 Look for the eggs. Summer is a good time to look for a monarch's eggs. Just duck your head low or gently lift the leaves of milkweed to look for eggs. This is where butterflies like

to lay the eggs. They are extremely tiny and are light or clear in color. You might bring along a magnifying glass to help you look. Do not touch the eggs, as they are very delicate.

4 If you find eggs, remember where you found them, and then go back in a couple of weeks to look for monarch caterpillars. The caterpillars are very distinct in color, in stripes of black, yellow, and white. They will spend days feeding on a milkweed plant as they grow bigger and bigger before they create a chrysalis.

5 Now that you know how important milkweed is to monarchs, it's time you plant some. Milkweed is a perennial, meaning it'll grow back year after year. While it used to be considered a weed by many, it's now a plant that a lot of people want in their backyard because it supports the monarchs. Get a plant or seeds to do your part.

Jack's Top Tips and Takeaways

- **Be careful and pay attention to detail.** If there are holes in milkweed, it could be a sign of caterpillars. But stay on the lookout because those caterpillars start out very small. Also, make sure that you are being careful around milkweed so you don't kill caterpillars.

- **Go out with a friend to look for monarchs or caterpillars.** It can be really challenging (and fun) to go out and look for monarch eggs or caterpillars. Bring along a friend or two and turn it into a challenge.

44

FIND AT LEAST THREE TRACES OF ANIMALS IN THE FOREST.

TRACKING ANIMALS CAN MEAN a lot of different things. Yes, it's one of the ways to find signs of animals in the wild, but there are many other ways, too. Here are several different animal signs you can look for. Your challenge is to find at least three of them during a single outing.

1 Find animal tracks. Keep your eyes on the ground to spot them. You're more likely to see tracks in areas that are soft or have impressional soil (like around ponds). When you find a track, notice its overall size and shape. How many impressions can you count? Does it have two distinct impressions, so it's likely a hoofed animal? Does it have three, so it might be a bird? How about five, indicating it might be a small mammal? If you find an animal track but can't ID it, try to take a picture of it so you can study it later.

2 Find animal scat. At first it might seem gross to go around looking for animal poop, but it's really pretty fascinating. Once you get a little practice, you'll easily be able to identify some basic animal scat like rabbit (small pellets), deer (larger and more oval in shape), and coyote (which can look a lot like dog poop). You'll soon find yourself fascinated by the different types of animal poop because it's a great way to find out what type of animal has been there.

3 Look for signs of animal homes. Animals like to keep their homes protected, so this isn't an easy one to accomplish. But you just need to know what to look for. Look up in trees for groupings of sticks that make a nest. Or look for holes in trees, caves, or the ground, serving as a protective den. You should never disturb an animal's home or get close to it, but if you think

you found something, keep an eye on it from a distance to see if you can spot something going in or coming out.

4 Look for signs of animal markings. The best place to look for this is on trees. Large animals like moose or deer will rub their antlers on trees, so you can see wear and tear down low on the tree. Birds like woodpeckers will also drill holes into trees, looking for insects or trying to make a home. Don't overlook the little signs, either. Insects like to eat into trees or leaves, and this should definitely count as one of your animal signs that you see.

5 Find animal hair, skin, or other signs. You can look for really big signs, like snakes that leave behind their skin from shedding. Or you can look for small signs, like a fluff of hair or even a tooth. These can all be fun to look for when you're out hiking in the woods.

Jack's Top Tips and Takeaways

- **Look for turtle shells in the wild.** It might be hard to believe, but you really can find turtle shells in the wild. They may be camouflaged among the leaves, but look closely for the pattern.

- **Pay attention to your surroundings.** Nature has some really cool historical stories to tell. Look for fossilized rocks that might house traces of animals from years ago. Or keep an eye out for the process of erosion at nearby streams.

= 45 =

DISCOVER AT LEAST THREE DIFFERENT CREATURES AT THE WATER.

GOING TO A NATURAL SOURCE OF WATER, like a lake, pond, or river, will almost guarantee you a glimpse of a wild animal. Here are five common creatures to look for when you're around a small body of water. The challenge here is to see at least three of them in one place, but an even bigger challenge would be to try to see four or five.

1 Look for birds fishing for food. You can look high in the treetops or low at the water's edge, but there will always be birds at the water. Some, like herons and egrets, will walk through the water, looking for small fish or other creatures to eat. Others, like kingfishers or swallows, will perch on trees along the edges so they can swoop down when they're ready. Then there are the ducks floating across the water. In all cases, birds can do a really good job of camouflaging themselves. Be patient.

2 Look for fish jumping through the water. If the water is clear enough, you can sometimes spot fish from up above as you walk on a bridge, boardwalk, or dock. If not, stay on the shore and wait for the fish to jump out of the water to show themselves.

3 Look for amphibians or reptiles hanging out along the edges. Frogs, toads, salamanders . . . these are all amphibians that will

hang along the edge of the water. They go on both land and water, so the best way for you to spot them is to focus on the shoreline. You can also spot reptiles, like snakes or lizards, in this same area.

4 Look for small mammals swimming or looking for food. Some of the most common small animals along the edge of the water include beavers, muskrats, otters, and raccoons. You might see them swimming through the water with just their heads poking up. Or they could be on the shoreline looking for something to eat.

5 Look for insects hopping or flying around. Many of the animals noted above are actively looking for insects to eat, and they go to the water because there are plenty there to choose from. Look for bees, dragonflies, and other small insects. If you're really lucky, you'll get to witness one of these other animals catch and eat an insect.

Jack's Top Tips and Takeaways

- **Wait it out.** You might not see something right away, but don't give up. You might even take along a book and spend some time there as you wait for animals to come up to the water. Being patient really can pay off.

- **Be on the lookout for larger animals.** Larger animals might come by the water to drink. They also might be there to catch insects or smaller animals. But they can be hard to see and won't come around if you're superloud, so always be quiet and on the lookout.

46

SEE AN ENDANGERED SPECIES.

THERE ARE PROBABLY A LOT MORE endangered species in your state and area than you realize. We think of endangered species as only existing in exotic, faraway places, but the truth is they're everywhere. It's important for us to know what species are endangered in our areas. This way, we can all do our part to help protect their habitat and help them survive for the future.

1 Learn what endangered species are around you. Do a Google search to find many websites dedicated to learning about endangered species. One of the best for the United States is the U.S. Fish and Wildlife Service. Go to fws.gov/endangered to search by your state for endangered animals. You'll be able to click on each animal listed to see what it looks like.

2 Learn more about the species and where to find them. Chances are, there will be several species listed as being endangered in your area, so focus on a few that are most interesting to you, and learn about them. What do they eat? Where do they live? What is their habitat like?

3 Now gather more information from wildlife experts who know more about the history of local endangered animals. They will likely be happy to talk to you about these animals and what you can do to help. And, because they're local, they will have the best tips on where to go to spot one of these animals, too.

4 Go out to find an endangered species. Now that you know more about a few of the endangered species in your area, go out and look for them. Be extremely careful that you do not do anything to damage the area or habitat in which these animals live. Observe from a distance, and don't interfere with their homes.

5 Do your part to help protect the habitat for the future. It's time to give back by doing what you can to protect these species. Do you want to help the bees? Plant bee-friendly plants. Are there fish or water animals on the list? Volunteer to help clean up area rivers. By finding small ways to help, you can help make a difference.

Jack's Top Tips and Takeaways

- **Do your research beforehand.** If you are looking for a certain species, then look up specific habitats they might have. You can also look up what sounds or tracks this certain species might make.

- **Go local.** If there is no opportunity for you to view an endangered animal in the wild, consider visitng one at your local zoo or nature center. By going to a zoo or a wildlife preserve, you can look at the endangered species up close. Often, the guides there can help you learn more, too.

≡ 47 ≡
SPOT AN OWL.

OWLS AREN'T REALLY SMALL BIRDS, but they are notoriously hard to find in the wild. You might hear them, especially at night, but seeing them offers a whole other challenge. If you know when and where to look, you can greatly increase your chances. Here's how.

1 Find out what owls are in your area and where they like to go. First, look in a bird book to learn about local owl varieties. For instance, there are nearly twenty types of owls in North America, but they like to be in secluded, hidden areas. Some of the most common owls to see in backyards or on hikes in the woods include barn, great-horned, eastern and western screech, great gray, elf, and saw-whet. Look at an owl's range map (found in bird books) to see if it's even in your area.

2 Start your search by looking up. Since many owls (but not all) like to nest in the woods, this is a good place to start. They like to be very high up, and they can easily blend into branches or tree bark because they are so still. Owls can sit without barely moving for hours, so binoculars can help you if you're scanning the trees.

3 Now try to find an owl by looking down. You're looking for an owl pellet, which is a small, round clump of matter consisting of parts of undigested food that owls cough up and spit out. Pellets will often include small mammal hair or bones because the owl has eaten its prey. This is one of the top signs that you've found an owl's roosting spot (aka, where it stays at night). So if you find owl pellets on the ground, center your search in this area.

4 Still no luck? Try your search at dawn or dusk. Because owls are nocturnal, it's not all that common to see them flying around during the day or moving much at all. They will often just hang out in the tops of trees and sleep, barely moving and making them impossible to see. For this reason, try going out at dawn or at dusk. Both are active times for owls as either they're about to wake up for the night to go hunting or they're coming back from exploring and hunting all night.

5 Finding an owl is a pretty amazing accomplishment, but now it's time to find another. Challenge yourself to spot a whole other species of owl. This could take months or years, but it's fun to always have another goal to tackle.

Jack's Top Tips and Takeaways

- **Know where to find snowy owls.** Snowy owls are a really amazing and fun type of owl to see, but they don't hang out in the woods. They like to hang out in open fields. And you would think it would be easy to find them in the wide open. This isn't the case, though. They blend into the background. They almost look like a plastic bag just blowing in the wind on a field.

- **Become familiar with owl characteristics prior to your search.** To help you find owls, research what noises they make, what types of prey they go after, and some interesting facts about their habitats. Being armed with this information prior to your search will make it easier to find an owl in the wild.

"IF PEOPLE CONCENTRATED ON THE REALLY IMPORTANT THINGS IN LIFE, THERE'D BE A SHORTAGE OF FISHING POLES."

—DOUG LARSON

Some people like fishing for the thrill of catching a big fish. For others, it's more about the peace and quiet of being in nature. No matter why you like to fish, it's a great hobby you can do just about anywhere. From ponds and lakes to streams that lead to the ocean, there are great fishing opportunities all over the world.

You've probably tried the basics with fishing, and now it's time to expand. Here are some great fishing experiences that everyone should have before they grow up.

48
LEARN HOW TO TAKE A FISH OFF THE HOOK.

IT'S EASY AND FUN TO CATCH A FISH, but it's a bit more challenging to take it off the hook and release it. It's mostly a matter of getting over your fear and just going for it, but there's some technique involved, too. Learn how to master this one all on your own.

1 Before you can learn to properly take a fish off a hook, you do have to get it on there first. Start with a small, barbless hook because this will likely have you catching a smaller fish. This is a safe hook for catch-and-release fishing, and the little fish are easier to learn on.

2 Leave your fish in water as long as possible until it's time to take them off the hook. Being out of the water is stressful for fish, and it makes them flop around more.

3 As you bring the fish out of the water, get a firm (but not too tight) grip around it. You want to have one hand covering the pectoral fins near the gills. If it's a small fish, you should be able to put your entire hand around the fish. It will wiggle around, so be ready for that. Even if it catches you off guard, try to stay calm and keep a good hold on it.

4 Now you have to remove the hook. Gently slip it out in the opposite direction it came through. Do not pull it up or out, as it could tear the mouth of the fish. If the hook doesn't come out right away, give it a little wiggle back and forth to help loosen it up. Move as quickly as possible, but keep your movements steady.

5 Once you get the fish off the hook, don't keep it out of the water too long. If you're going to take a picture, make it quick. Then release it back into the water. It will be very happy!

Jack's Top Tips and Takeaways

- **If you have a problem, get help immediately.** If the fish swallows the hook, you will need help right away. Be extremely gentle and careful when pulling out the hook. In some cases, you might even need pliers. If pliers are needed, ask an adult with some experience for help.

- **Keep yourself and the fish safe and healthy.** If you see the fish flopping a lot, you should put it back into the water to make sure it can breathe and stay alive. Also, be careful with your grip. You should use your fingers to flatten the fins so they don't poke you. In some cases, their sharp fins can draw blood.

49

FISH FOR SALMON.

SALMON IS ONE OF THE MOST POPULAR fish for anglers. Since salmon are seasonal (they migrate) and are only in certain areas, fishing for them makes for a fun challenge. They also have a reputation for putting up a good fight on the line, making the "chase" for one really invigorating. If fishing for salmon is on your list, try these tips.

1 Go to the right places. To catch salmon, you have to go to certain places in the United States, like Maine on the East Coast, the Great Lakes in the Midwest, and states like Washington and Alaska in the West. Unless you live near these areas, you'll likely have to travel to get to the best places to fish for salmon.

2 Be sure to go during the right time of year. Since salmon are a migrating fish, and you'll have the best luck catching them when they're on the move, spring tends to be the best time. However, it's good to do research first. Google "fish for salmon in Maine" (or Alaska, Washington, Oregon, etc.) and look for a chart that will show you when is the best time to go for that area.

3 Have the right equipment to catch salmon. You need the right pole, line weight, and lure to catch salmon. If you're unsure, it's definitely worth finding a guide or someone to go with you who regularly fishes for salmon and who can point out the right gear for you.

4 Learn the art of drift fishing. You can drift fish while using a fly-fishing rod or another kind of rod. It's basically a technique that lets your line drift along in the water. Since you're often fishing for salmon in moving water, like streams or rivers, you cast out your line and then let it float through the water from upstream to downstream. This is an easy way to fish for salmon, and, by moving along with them, it's a lot more natural. Then you're more likely to get them to hit on your lure.

5 Don't give up. Salmon fishing is not easy, but it's such an awesome experience once you finally catch one. If you don't succeed at first, don't give up. You might just need a different technique or some advice from a regular angler. Or you might need to go to a different location or try a new time of year. Keep after it until you achieve it.

Jack's Top Tips and Takeaways

- **Take a road trip.** One of the best places to go fishing for salmon is in Alaska. Alaska has a lot of rivers and lakes and two oceans. The Pacific Northwest is also a good area for salmon. I want to go to Alaska someday to fish for salmon because it seems extremely fun.

- **Have patience.** Patience is needed for all kinds of fishing, and it's especially the case with salmon. Don't get discouraged. Keep repeating your actions over and over again until you finally have some success.

- **Waders are a good thing to have for salmon fishing.** They're also fun to have because you get to walk into the water, which is a really cool experience. Waders will allow you to stay dry while also getting closer to the action.

50

TRY FLY FISHING.

MANY TIMES, PEOPLE ARE INTIMIDATED by fly fishing. If you've seen pictures or videos of someone fly fishing, with the giant waving of the rod and the line dancing in the air, it looks pretty difficult. Yes, certain types of fly fishing can be involved and take years of practice to master, but this shouldn't stop you from giving it a try. Just start with the basics.

1 Get yourself a fly rod. There really is no way around this one. You do need some special equipment to try fly fishing, and this is one of them. If you're unsure about making a full investment into a fly rod, try renting one or going with a fly-fishing guide who can really show you the ropes.

2 Learn to tie flies. Flies are the bait you use for fly fishing, and almost all fly fishermen and fisherwomen learn how to tie them onto their line as part of learning this sport. You really have to see this in action and then do it yourself. If you know someone who can teach you how to tie a fly, this is best. Otherwise, look up a video on YouTube or check out howtoflyfish.orvis.com.

3 Hit the waters at the right time of year. Locals will know what the fishing is like at any time of year, but spring is usually a good time to go. Keep in mind that most fly fishing happens in moving water, like streams or rivers, so you want the water to be active but not too fast or it won't be safe.

4 Start small, casting a little at a time. You don't have to look like the pictures or videos of people fly fishing when you first get started. In fact, it might take you a long time to look like that. So start small by making short casts into the water. It's almost

like you're gently tossing the line out and then letting it float or move downstream with the natural movement of the water.

5 As you master your technique, build on it. Go a little farther and a little higher each time. Eventually, you will start to have a really smooth technique, one where your casting almost looks like a continuous wave, going back and forth in the water. Learn how to detect what a bite (or strike) feels like so you know when to jerk the rod up and start reeling in the fish.

Jack's Top Tips and Takeaways

- **Don't stay in one place too long.** You should always cast in one spot for a little while, but don't stay for too long. If the fish aren't biting in one spot, keep moving to try different spots.

- **Let the river carry the fly naturally.** You don't want to pull against the water. Just toss your line in and let it naturally go with the motion. This allows the fish to follow along, as they're going with the motion of the water, too.

- **Trout, in particular, don't like fast-moving current.** This means finding spots can be a bit tricky, but once you do, the fish will start biting. Look for sections of the water where rocks slow the current down. These are good spots to try.

51

LEARN HOW TO IDENTIFY DIFFERENT TYPES OF FISH.

AS YOU GO FISHING AND GET MORE EXPERIENCE, you're probably going to want to know what you're seeing and catching. It also makes it more fun because it'll help you build up your list of fish you've caught and fish you want to catch.

1 Learn the most common fish in your area. Find this by doing a Google search of "most common fish in _____" with the blank being your state. You'll likely find an article or a diagram that highlights the most common fish. If you do find a diagram, try to then do an image search for actual images. This will allow you to compare an illustration to a picture, which will help you when you're out fishing in the wild.

2 Now learn the rare fish in your area. Go beyond identifying the most common fish in your area and learn about a few that occur rarely. This way, if you come across something you don't recognize while fishing, you'll have a better idea of what you might have. If you have trouble researching rare fish in your area online, look for a fish book at your local library.

3 Put your skills to the test as you're out fishing. Each time you get an up-close look at a fish, try to ID it correctly. You will slowly start to build your knowledge and skills. Learn how to recognize certain fish by their size and shape. This will allow you to ID a fish in the water, too.

4 When you come upon fish that you can't ID, pay attention to detail. The size of fins, the overall coloring, and other small details can make a huge difference. You should also try to take a picture so you can then compare it to photos online.

5 Once you master identifying fish in your area, now try to ID fish in other areas. When you go fishing at a new place, learn about the most common fish and pay attention to those same details as before. There are so many fish in the world, and they can vary a great deal from one region to the next, but keep growing those skills.

Jack's Top Tips and Takeaways

- **Go to an aquarium or zoo to help identify fish.** Zoos and aquariums usually always have a local fish section. This section shows pictures, gives information about the fish, and shows how to identify the fish. It will also usually have the families of fish. You can learn a lot about different fish this way.

- **Pay attention to detail.** Fish in the same families will be similar in shape, but each species will have unique coloring and patterns. A good example of this is the trout family. If you focus in on the rainbow trout and the brown trout, you can see that they have very similar shape, but the way they're colored is extremely different from each other.

52
FIND YOUR OWN BAIT FOR FISHING.

WHY USE PLASTIC WORMS OR BUY SOME at the store when you could dig up your own worms instead? This challenge will get you outside digging in the dirt just like you did when you were a little kid. Then you can use those worms to go fishing.

1 Find a good place to dig for worms. A garden makes a great worm bed, but you don't want to disturb your plants. Plus, worms add such good nutrients to the soil, so leave them be in the garden. Try a different place in your yard where it's OK to dig.

2 Try to dig right after a light rainfall. Earthworms like to crawl to the surface of the ground when it rains because they are after the damp moisture. Sometimes you'll even see earthworms all over the yard after a spring rain.

3 Use a big shovel and dig as deep as you can. If you use a small shovel, you have a greater risk of cutting the earthworm in half. So use a big shovel and get a huge scoop or even a few huge scoops. Then get your hands dirty and sort through the soil a little bit at a time. Earthworms will try to hide. Break up the soil gently as you go.

4 Put the worms in a dark, cool container for storage. A plastic bucket or small container will work, but make sure you punch holes so the worms can breathe. Keep them in here until it's time to go fishing. If you aren't using them within a day or two, it's best to release them and wait until you are ready for fishing.

5 Put a worm on the hook and cast your line into the water. Just like you would a regular earthworm you buy from a store, pull your worm out and get it ready to cast in the water. Depending on the size of the worm, you might pinch the worm in half for fishing.

Jack's Top Tips and Takeaways

- **Look for worms in shady areas.** Worms like being cool and shaded from the sun. If you look under a shrub or a structure, there will probably be a lot more fresh worms to use for bait.

- **Worms aren't the only bait that you can use.** You can also catch grasshoppers and other bugs to use as bait. The fish will love them just as much as they do the worm.

- **Be sure to keep the bait in a secure spot.** Worms, grasshoppers, and other bugs will not like being eaten. So they will probably try to escape. Keep whatever you're using as bait in a good storage area, with air holes, so they don't get away and they can breathe.

⚡ 53 ⚡
GO DEEP-SEA FISHING.

DEEP-SEA FISHING IS ONE OF the most memorable, challenging, and thrilling types of fishing you can do. It involves going out into the ocean to catch huge fish, like swordfish, halibut, and tuna. You will catch things out in deep waters that you can only dream of catching inland.

1 Identify a place you want to go. There are many options for deep-sea fishing. Just pick a place along the ocean. Some of the most popular areas include the coast of California, all along the Gulf from Texas to Florida, and pretty much all up and down the East Coast. But, really, anywhere along the ocean will likely have deep-sea-fishing options.

2 Find a reputable guide or company to go with. They will have the right boat, equipment, and knowledge to make sure you have a good trip. Not all guides are created equal, so reach out and ask questions before your trip. Be sure you find one that is good with kids or teens. They should be friendly and willing to answer questions.

3 Ask the guide for their advice for when to go, what you need to bring, and so on. They will likely provide everything you need, but they can give you advice on other things, like whether or not you need a fishing license, when to show up, and many other details.

4 Hit the deep sea and listen to your guide at all times. It's important that you show up on time so you can go through all

the basics and get started right away. You will probably be eager to get started and catch fish, but try to be patient. The guides know the area and waters better than anyone, so let them lead. It's OK to tell them what you're hoping to fish for and what you're hoping to get out of the trip, but then put your trip in their hands.

5 Don't forget to enjoy everything that comes with deep-sea fishing. Look for dolphins, whales, and other sea life as you're out and about on the water. Breathe in that sea air. Ask questions about boat life and the history of the area. By going with a local guide, you really will get the most out of the experience.

Jack's Top Tips and Takeaways

- **Avoid motion sickness.** Deep-sea fishing is an experience you'll probably remember for a lifetime, but one experience you don't want is motion sickness. Try taking ginger or a motion sickness pill before you get on the boat. There are also motion sickness bracelets you can wear while out on the water.

- **Make your trip right for you.** Everyone has their own preference on how long they want to be out fishing. There's no right or wrong amount of time. A lot of places will have half-day or full-day options. Pick the amount of time that works for you.

- **Catch your dream fish.** If you are looking to fish for a certain type of fish, do some research. Some companies might specialize in certain fish, like tuna, halibut, or some other fish. If the type of fish you're looking to catch matters to you, then choose carefully.

BACKYARDING

"ADVENTURE IS WORTHWHILE IN ITSELF."

—AMELIA EARHART

You don't always have to take a trip or go somewhere to have a great experience with nature and the outdoors. Sometimes you just have to step outside in your own backyard. Or if you don't have much of a backyard, explore your park or neighborhood instead.

This chapter is filled with activities that you can complete by simply walking outside. Many of them you might recognize or have even done, but don't let that stop you from tackling them again. These are the kinds of things we should do over and over again for epic backyard adventures.

54
CREATE A BUG HOME
IN YOUR BACKYARD.

BUGS ARE AN IMPORTANT PART of backyards. Ladybugs, spiders, dragonflies, bees, and other insects are considered good backyard bugs. They help get rid of the other, not-so-good bugs, and they can also be really helpful to plants and your garden. By encouraging these bugs in your backyard, you're promoting a healthy backyard.

1 Find a good spot for your bug home. You might naturally already have a good spot for bugs in your backyard. For instance, if you have a corner of your yard with a tree stump or an area where there are rocks or sticks, this is perfect. Instead of clearing these areas out, pile up the items instead. This will naturally create little nooks and crannies for bugs to go.

2 Gather materials. If you don't have a spot already with materials readily available, then go ahead and gather the materials, either in your own backyard or during a hike. Sticks, small rocks, and other items can be put together to create a bug habitat. Do a search for "bug hotel" online and you'll see how you can arrange sticks together to make it. When completed, it's kind of a cool art piece, and it's like a Welcome sign to bugs.

3 Stop using pesticides and other items that might get in the way of your efforts. There are many bug killers out there, but it's best to avoid using them completely if you want to promote

a bug-friendly yard. If you really need a spray to deal with something like weeds, then try to look for an organic option.

4 Try making a bee home, too. This is similar to the bug hotel, but this time, search online specifically for how to make a bee home. Since the bee population has been on the decline and we greatly need our bees to pollinate plants in the garden, this is definitely important.

5 Leave it alone. Once you get your bug house or bug area set, it's time to let it be. Resist the temptation to check on it, move things around, or get too close to it. The bugs need time to move in, so it's important that you don't mess with it too much.

Jack's Top Tips and Takeaways

- **Add plants.** To get started, look for bee-friendly plants and flowers good for butterflies. At the garden center, the plants are usually marked in this way. Try to get a good variety to appeal to a lot of different types of bugs.

- **Put up a sign.** Some people have no idea what a bug-friendly area might look like. To recognize your space, put up a sign. This will help others see what you're doing, and it might even inspire them to create their own area.

- **Try making a fairy garden.** These are so popular right now—there are miniature accessories to put in a garden so it looks like a fairy lives there. You can find these items at garden centers or craft stores. You could also invent your own. It's a fun way to decorate your space.

55

BUILD A BACKYARD FORT.

IF YOU'VE NEVER HAD A BACKYARD FORT, it's time to create one. Or, if you already have one, consider renovating it or adding on to it. The backyard fort will never get old, and it can provide hours of entertainment. Time to get building!

1 Find a good location for your fort. If you have a great tree for a tree fort or an old building to make your own, then you're all set. However, if you're starting from scratch, look for a spot *under* a tree. This will give you solid protection from the weather.

2 Start by creating a basic fort with a sheet or a tarp. You'll need something to put your material over, like a clothesline, tree branch, or outdoor chairs. This approach is similar to a blanket fort you might build inside your home by lining up chairs in a square and then putting the blanket over them. A variation on this approach is to make a hula hoop fort using five hula hoops (do a YouTube search for "hula hoop fort" for step-by-step instructions) and covering it with a sheet for the ultimate fort getaway.

3 Take it to the next level by creating your own structure. This might seem intimidating, but basic designs can be put together with hammer, nails, and inexpensive wood. You can find plenty of plans online. Make this a weekend project, and get the whole family involved.

4 Decide what your fort will be used for and decorate it. Does it need a cooler inside to store snacks? Does it need books because you go there to relax and read? Perhaps you want to add

a blanket and a pillow to the inside so you're comfy. This is your chance to really make your fort your own.

5 Give your fort a sign. Every good space has a sign. Use some recycled wood or cardboard, and then paint your sign. Give your fort a name, too. Add a couple of nails to the back of the sign and wrap wire around them so it has something to hang by.

Jack's Top Tips and Takeaways

- **Try using a tent.** Sometimes it can be expensive and hard to get all the materials needed to create a fort. Or you might not have the time or money to look for the right materials. So, instead, get a tent and set it up in your backyard. Then you can add something unique to make it your own.

- **Try cardboard.** You might think of cardboard as being flimsy, but, with some duct tape, it can make for a sturdy fort. Plus, it's inexpensive. Keep an eye out for a large cardboard box package and save the box for your fort. Just keep the cardboard fort out of water, which will make it soggy and smelly.

- **Use a fence as one of the fort walls.** Forts can be a lot of work. To cut down on the time and effort, take advantage of positioning your fort against a fence or wall. This will make the construction easier because you only have to construct three walls.

56
FLY A KITE IN YOUR NEIGHBORHOOD.

FLYING A KITE IS ONE OF THOSE THINGS that you really want to do once you see someone else doing it. It looks like so much fun as the kite soars through the air buoyantly. Now, you might not be able to fly a kite in your own backyard, but this is still a great challenge to tackle right in your own neighborhood.

1 Find an open field or area. When flying kites, you want to be careful that there are not power lines nearby or even close. If you can be near a big lake, ocean, or other body of water, this will also help because it's usually windier in these areas.

2 Go on a windy day. Even if you do go to the ocean, you can't always count on it being good kite-flying weather. Keep an eye on the weather, and look for winds that are in the 5 to 15 mph range for smaller kites and 10 to 25 mph for bigger ones.

3 Learn how to give your kite a head start. First, stand with your back to the wind. Next, hold your kite up high (with lots of extra line already pulled out) and wait for a gust of wind to come along. As it does, take off running in the opposite direction and let go of the kite. If the wind is right, the kite should go up right away. Then turn around and continue letting line out so the kite goes higher and higher into the air.

4 Observe the wind around you, and adjust as needed. Let the kite go back and forth, moving naturally with the wind. If you see the kite start to fall or falter because of loss of wind, then give

it another firm pull up and toward you, and maybe even take off running again. This can help the kite stay high in the sky. Then, once it's high and strong, you can have a little more fun with the kite by trying to get it to dive, zip, and scoop.

5 As you master one kite, graduate yourself to the next level. There are definitely different difficulty levels of kites. Once you get through a basic one and you have a good feel for it, move on to another one. This will likely mean purchasing a larger, longer kite.

Jack's Top Tips and Takeaways

- **Find a kite shop near you.** You might have a kite shop near you, but you never even knew it. (Toy stores often have kites, too.) Find one in your area, and pay it a visit. When you talk to the workers, you might learn a lot about different types of kites or the best places in the area to fly your kite.

- **Make your own kite.** Did you know you can make your own kite? All you need to start is some plastic, and then add sticks or wooden rods. You'll need string and either tape or glue to make it all go together, as well. Find a how-to video on YouTube for instructions.

- **Fly a kite at the beach.** It's such a cool experience to fly your kite on a beach, and you may find you're not the only kite flyer on the sand. If you go on vacation to a beach area, you'll probably find kite stands or shops nearby where you can buy or rent one to fly.

≡ 57 ≡
WATCH A METEOR SHOWER.

METEOR SHOWERS ARE A COOL, sometimes unpredictable, natural phenomenon that occurs in the night sky, and to watch one with your own eyes is a pretty amazing experience. You just need to know when and where to look and do a little planning to catch one of these awesome moments for yourself.

1 Know what meteor showers are. A lot of us know meteors as "shooting stars" at night, but they are actually space rocks falling through, well, space. These rocks fall so fast that the air around them seems to be glowing. This is why it looks like a shooting star across the sky. During certain times of year, more meteors fall than during other times, thus producing a meteor "shower" in the sky.

2 Learn the best time of year to view them. Scientists have gotten very good about predicting meteor showers. Google the current year and the phrase "meteor showers" to get a really solid calendar of when you should be on the lookout.

3 Go to a good viewing spot. One of the best parts of observing meteor showers is that you don't need anything special to

do it—just a clear night and a dark sky. Then you can sit out on a blanket and wait for the stars to fall (even though you know they really aren't stars).

4 Find a local astronomy club to make the experience even more enjoyable. They will often hold watch parties, which they'll open up to the public. This is a good time to get to know others in your area who are into astronomy. Plus, even though you don't need special equipment to see meteor showers, they'll have cool telescopes to give you a whole new experience.

5 Try to see a meteor shower in every season. Now this will be a challenge because the weather and timing won't always work out, but it's fun to attempt it.

Jack's Top Tips and Takeaways

- **Stay up late.** Sometimes meteor showers are heavier during certain times of the night. Scientists have been able to predict peak times, so you may be able to get this information online if you see there is going to be one in your area. This is also a good excuse to stay up late.

- **Spend some time on this challenge.** If you don't see a bunch of showers right away, don't give up. It's easy to miss meteor showers because they happen so quickly. So spend at least an hour outside during a peak meteor shower time.

CHASE THE GLOW OF FIREFLIES IN YOUR YARD.

THIS ONE IS GOING TO BE A LOT EASIER for those of you in the East versus those of you in the West. This is because there are different species of fireflies (also called lightning bugs) in the two areas. The eastern species are well known for lighting up backyards right around dusk, while western species don't glow in the same way, and so you're not as likely to see them glowing in yards. If you do happen to live in the West, you might have to do this one while visiting the East.

1 Know the right time of year to look for fireflies. Late spring is especially popular, as is early summer. Since male fireflies in the East use their glow to attract females, early in the season, when the courtship is at its peak, is best.

2 It's common to put on bug spray when you're going to be in the backyard at night, but you don't want anything that could affect firefly health. They are actually a population on the decline. So avoid mosquito spray with pesticides. Having it on your hands or arms can harm them. Try a natural spray instead, or hold off until you're done chasing them.

3 Want to catch fireflies? You'll need the right kind of container. A mason jar or plastic container will work just fine, but definitely be sure to punch holes in the lid so the bugs can breathe.

4 Be sure to go at the right time of night. Fireflies tend to come out when it's just starting to get dark. So be ready for them. Get into position and turn off your porch lights to help attract them.

5 Watch them glow, and then let them go. It's easy to forget about having a bug in the jar, but catch and release is very important. Once you've seen them glow in your jar, it's time to let them go on their way.

Jack's Top Tips and Takeaways

- **Make it competitive.** Have a friendly little firefly competition to see who can get the most glow. Put a time limit on the clock and then set out catching fireflies. You might even take a little video at the end to see the glows and compare.

- **Don't always chase.** If you stand still, fireflies may come to you instead of you going to them. This is because you'll blend into the nature around you, and they're more likely to come up or even land on you.

- **Get low and look up.** Sometimes fireflies are hard to see, especially if you're looking straight across or down into the grass. Try getting low to the ground and looking up at the sky. This will help you pick out the fireflies easier.

59
LEARN HOW TO ATTRACT BATS.

THE BAT IS A FASCINATING MAMMAL that many people will never see because it rarely comes out during the day. Even though some people are afraid of bats, they are a useful animal that can bring a lot of benefits to your backyard—like eating bad bugs or helping to pollinate your plants. Consider helping them out by making your backyard bat-friendly.

1 Stop using most pesticides on your yard. This can be challenging, but it really is necessary to attract beneficial bugs and animals like bats to your yard. Yes, you sometimes want to use pesticides in certain areas or when dealing with a stubborn weed, but try to avoid blanketing your yard in pesticides. It will negatively affect the wildlife in the area.

2 Learn how to make a bat house for your yard. You can find so many plans for a bat house online, and Bat Con International (batcon.org) is a good place to go if you're just getting started. In addition to getting instructions for creating a bat house, you'll learn a lot of useful information about bats in general. (You can also buy a bat house if you don't want to make it yourself.)

3 Hang your bat house in the right spot. Bats prefer a home that hangs on a structure of some sort, and it's usually pretty high up. As a good rule of thumb, put the house in a spot that gets at least 6 hours of sunlight. Bats are mammals, after all, so that sunlight and warmth is a good thing.

4 Add plants that will attract bats. Yes, there are plants that attract bats! Look for night-blooming plants, like evening primrose, yucca, moonflower, and others. You can also do some additional plant research online by searching for "plants for a moon garden."

5 Spread the word to others that bats are good creatures. Even though the reputation of bats is slowly changing, it still has a long way to go. You can help by telling people how cool bats are. Little things like this can really help positively get the word out.

Jack's Top Tips and Takeaways

- **Look for activity around the opening of the house.** Bat houses have openings in the bottom. This isn't typical when compared to a birdhouse, so you have to get used to looking low instead of high.

- **Go out at dusk.** An easy way to spot a bat is to go out right at dusk. For bats, this is a prime time to eat insects.

- **Don't be scared.** If you see swooping bats, you shouldn't be afraid. They aren't flying at you; they're looking for insects. Don't run. Just stay still and watch them fly.

60
LEARN BACKYARD YOGA.

YOUR BACKYARD CAN BE A GREAT PLACE to take a break, relax, and even get a workout in. With yoga, you can do all of these at once. Ready to stretch and increase your flexibility? Let's take on this challenge.

1 Find a good place to practice. This will depend on the time of day that you go out to do yoga. If you go out in the morning, you might find a place where the sun is just starting to peek through the tree line. If you go out in the middle of the day, you might want to find a little bit of shade to protect yourself from the heat and becoming sunburned.

2 Learn some basic poses. Search online for "yoga poses for kids," and you'll get several diagrams that show you poses like tree, warrior, mountain, cobra, boat, and down dog. You can try these on your own, or, for more step-by-step instruction, look up a yoga routine on YouTube to try, as well. Start small, around 5 to 10 minutes of workouts.

3 If you have a yoga mat, take it outside. Otherwise, a towel will work, too. Don't forget to dress in comfortable clothes and take water along. Before you start any poses, be sure to do some stretches to warm up your muscles.

4 Put a yoga schedule together. Part of doing yoga is actually making it a habit. You don't have to do yoga every single day for an hour or more. Instead, just make a loose schedule to try yoga two or three times a week. It can help you relax, clear your mind, and even give you more focus.

5 Invite friends to try yoga with you. Now that you're practicing yoga (saying you're "practicing" makes you sound legit), share it with others. Invite some friends over, or get your parent or sibling to join you.

Jack's Top Tips and Takeaways

- **Try it anytime.** Outdoor yoga isn't just a summer activity. With the right kind of clothing, you can try it year-round.

- **Download an app.** If you look up "yoga" in the app store, you will find lots of different options. Many of them are free. Browse through to find the right one for you—be it beginner yoga, more advanced, or specific poses—and give one of these a try. The apps will show you the right technique and how the pose should look.

- **Time to breathe.** A big part of yoga is learning how to breathe. Here's an insider tip: Count to get your breathing down and to make sure you're taking deep breaths and are not going too fast.

61
LEARN HOW TO FIND THE NORTH STAR FROM YOUR BACKYARD.

THE NORTH STAR IS AN IMPORTANT STAR in the sky because it's a center point in the Northern Hemisphere. Not only is it one of the brightest stars in the sky (but not *the* brightest), it represents the North Celestial Pole. This means everything else will move and shift around it, but it stays in one spot. So it's helpful for you to locate the star in your own backyard.

1 Try to find the North Star by starting with the Big Dipper. This is one of the easiest constellations to find in the night sky, so many people use it to find the North Star. Once you locate it, find the corner of the Big Dipper that makes up the spoon. This start points directly to the North Star.

2 Try to find it with the Little Dipper. Find the very end (the handle) of the Little Dipper, which often is upside-down. This is the North Star.

3 Use an app to find it instead. Technology can be a pretty great thing, and there are plenty of constellation apps you can download to help you learn and locate stars and constellations. These apps work as a compass of sorts. You just have to hold your device up to the sky, and they'll help you navigate to the North Star.

4 Now that you've learned how to find the North Star, learn about the other constellations around it. This will change with the season and where exactly the constellations are in the sky, but learning to recognize the North Star is a good way to expand your knowledge about constellations.

5 Share your knowledge with others. Teach a sibling, parent, cousin, or friend how to find the North Star. You can give them all of your tricks, and then feel good knowing that you're passing on some nature knowledge to others.

Jack's Top Tips and Takeaways

- **Make it official.** If you're going to learn about the North Star, you might as well learn its name. The official name is Polaris.

- **Look for it year-round.** Not all stars or constellations have good visibility all year. But this is one you can find in all seasons. Challenge yourself to find it in every single season this year.

- **It's not so bright.** Even though the North Star seems like the brightest star—and many people think this— it's actually not. In fact, it's only about the fiftieth brightest star in the sky. The brightest star award goes to Sirius. It's part of the constellation Canis Major.

WATER ADVENTURING

"WATER PROVIDES THE MOST PROFOUND SHORTCUT TO HAPPINESS OUT THERE."

—WALLACE J. NICHOLS

A day on the water is a great way to get up close and personal with nature. There's something awesome about being on a lake, river, or pond that a swimming pool just can't compete with. You can explore remote areas and visit unique places. And best of all? You're sharing those waters with the birds, insects, fish, and all other wildlife in the area.

For this reason, it's important to remember to be respectful of water areas, and do your part to keep them clean and free of litter.

This chapter is filled with activities that you can complete by simply walking outside. Many of them you might recognize or have even done before, but don't let that stop you from tackling them again. These are the kinds of things we should do over and over again for epic water adventures. Don't forget to wear a life jacket for all of these adventures.

⋹ 62 ⋺
TRY PADDLEBOARDING.

START PRACTICING YOUR BALANCE because you'll need it with paddleboarding. This stand-up water sport has been growing in popularity, and it's a perfect mix of challenging and relaxing.

1 Find a paddleboard. They can be pretty expensive to buy on your own, so before you make that big purchase, you might want to see where you can rent one to try out. You can also look for paddleboarding adventures to sign up for in your area.

2 Practice and build up your balance. You can figure out balance and where to stand on your paddleboard before you ever get on the water. If you take a class, your instructor will likely have you do this before you go out. You want to stand toward the middle of your paddleboard with your knees slightly bent. You can even practice your paddleboard stroke, dipping your single oar from one side to the other.

3 Find a calm body of water. When you're first starting to paddleboard, don't go on a rapid river or water that is really choppy. Instead, start on a calm body of water so you can get a good feel for balancing on water.

4 You don't have to start out standing right away. In fact, when you first put your paddleboard in the water, you'll likely start out seated or on your belly. Get a feel for the movement and using your paddle first. Then move to your knees and practice this for

a while. Finally, when you are ready to try standing, stand up on one foot and then the other. This motion should be smooth—not too slow and not too quick. Remember, you're going to that standing position with your knees slightly bent. Don't lock those legs because you want to be able to quickly adjust at any time.

5 As you get more comfortable on your board, build up the speed a little at a time. Remember, it's OK to drop back down to your knees or even fall. You're just falling into water, after all. Just climb back on your board and go again. You'll get the hang of it and will soon be paddling through the water at a quick speed.

Jack's Top Tips and Takeaways

- **Challenge yourself.** If you really want a challenge, try paddleboarding with a dog. Yes, people really do this! It'll be tough to get the balance right. But for the right kind of dog, they'll enjoy the experience.

- **Look for calm water.** If you're just getting started, go early in the morning or in the evening when waters tend to be calmer. It's also just a nice time to go because you might be able to catch the sunrise or sunset.

- **Check your form.** If you're having a tough time, be sure to recheck your form. For instance, your feet should be shoulder-width apart. If they're too wide or too close together, it might throw off your balance.

63

FLOAT DOWN A RIVER.

HOT SUMMER DAYS OFFER up a great opportunity to sit back, relax, and enjoy your surroundings . . . all while floating on an inner tube. This activity is better enjoyed with family and friends, so gather up a few and find a river to conquer.

1 Find the perfect river for a float. Remember, a big part of this task is floating leisurely—it's not a race! If a river moves too quickly, you'll probably want to skip it. Instead, look for a river that has a slow flow to it.

2 Pick up inner tubes or rent them from a local place. There are a lot of float companies out there who have already scouted out great places to go. Use these places, their knowledge, and their equipment to have the best experience possible.

3 Find a way to bring along snacks and drinks. If you're floating in a tube, you have to be a little creative about where to put items like your phone, camera, and food. Waterproof gear and bags are a must. Look for a floating cooler to take along with you on your float. All you have to do is tie it to one of your tubes (so it doesn't float away). You'll be glad you have it when you take a snack break.

4 Pace yourself, and enjoy the river as you go. You might be tempted to take off and just go as fast as you can, but this should really be a slow, easygoing ride. If you find that you're moving too fast, then stay out of the middle part of the river where the current moves the fastest. Go to the edges instead.

5 Don't forget to get a ride to and from your adventure. This is an important one. Since you will be floating down a river, you will not start and finish at the same place. Plan for this by having

someone drop you off, and then make a plan to meet at a certain point a few hours later. (Make sure everyone is 100 percent clear where this is so there's no confusion.) This is another reason to use a float or tour company, because they will drop you off and pick you up when you're done.

Jack's Top Tips and Takeaways

- **Don't forget the sunscreen.** Even if it's cloudy, you don't want to forget your sunscreen. Put it on before you get on the water for the best chance of it staying on all day.

- **Watch the weather.** If it's superhot out, the middle of the day might not be the best time to go out on the river. Pay attention to the highs and lows in the weather forecast, and adjust accordingly.

- **Keep it safe.** If you have a phone, electronics, or other valuables, be sure to keep your items in a waterproof bag.

64
TRAVEL BY CANOE.

CANOES HAVE BEEN A MODE OF TRAVEL for hundreds and hundreds of years, and they're still a great way to get around on the water today. They might not have a motor or be trendy, like paddleboards, but everyone should experience canoe travel at some point in their life. Just pick a destination and go.

1 Find a canoe. They can be big and bulky, and for this reason, you might be better off finding a canoe already on the water that you can go directly to. This way, you don't have to worry about loading it up on a car. You'll simply be able to load it up and go. Some outfitters supply canoes for rent that are ready to go for you.

2 Recruit a canoe partner. Since canoes are so big and bulky, it really helps to have a partner to help you paddle. Most canoes are designed to have someone in the front and someone in the back. Just make sure you have two paddles. This way you can both help paddle, rotating from one side to the other.

3 Practice on a small, flat area of water. It can definitely take some time to get the hang of paddling, and to learn how to paddle with another person. Start by practicing this with your canoe buddy in a small area. Work on developing a good system for your paddling to complement each other. This will help you move through the water faster and more smoothly.

4 Plan a bigger canoe trip. Now that you've got the hang of it, plan a longer, bigger canoe adventure. Find a good canoe place to go to, and challenge yourself to go for several miles or hours. This will really make you feel like you're conquering a big goal.

5 Pack up and go. Don't forget to take snacks, water, and even a basic first-aid kit. You'll probably want to start your paddle early in the day just to give yourself extra time to explore the waterway. If you're borrowing a canoe or renting from a place, be sure to ask them for tips about when and where to go. You might even need a reservation—planning ahead never hurts.

Jack's Top Tips and Takeaways

- **Test out paddles.** Some people like a paddle that is long while others like shorter ones. You will want to try out different paddle lengths to see what feels most comfortable. To do this, squat or sit down and put the paddle across your body. How does it feel? When you dip the blade in the water, does it feel good?

- **Have a plan.** Before you go, consult a map of the area, if one is available. Waterways start to look the same after a while, and you can easily get lost. Find markers to watch for along the way.

- **Stay steady.** When paddling, try to stay in the center of the canoe. You might get tempted to lean in one direction or the other as you try to turn and maneuver. But this could throw you off balance.

⭒ 65 ⭒
KAYAK ACROSS A LAKE.

KAYAKING IS ONE OF THE BEST WAYS to explore all the nooks and crannies of lakes, rivers, and ponds. Since kayaks are shallow and lightweight, they are easy to maneuver and can even go in shallow waters that other boat traffic can't reach. Once you get the hang of them, which doesn't take much, they'll easily become one of your favorite ways to get out and explore nature.

1 Find a kayak to use. Kayaks have been growing in popularity, and they're actually pretty affordable, too. Ask around to see if you have any friends with kayaks or with access to kayaks. If not, do a search for kayaks in your area (or wherever you're going). There will likely be lots of options for rentals. You can rent a single-person kayak or a two-person one. There are kayaks with seats in the boat, with "skirts" covering the seat, or sit-on-top kayaks that leave your lower body exposed. Whatever vessel you use, be sure to learn all of its functions. It is also a good idea to take a safety course.

2 Tackle a pond or small lake. With kayaks, the best way to get out and get the hang of it is to get on the water. There is definitely some balance involved, but you have to feel it for yourself. Some people worry a lot about tipping over, but it's not actually that big of a deal. You just swim out of your kayak and then flip it back over. For kayaks with skirts on them, there's a

wet release tab at the front end of the skirt that, while you're submerged, you can pull back. This releases the skirt and allows you to swim out of the kayak to then flip it back over.

3 Next, tackle a large lake. With the small lake or pond, you'll probably be able to see everywhere from one spot. There won't be many areas to explore. But when you move to a large lake, you'll be able to go around bends or in little offshoot areas to see and do more. Set a goal (either distance or time limit), and then conquer it on this large lake.

4 Now, tackle a slow-moving river. This is a little trickier because you'll eventually have to go against the natural flow of the river. This can be tiring. Sure, it's easy to go with the flow, but then when you turn around and go upriver, it's much harder. You might want to practice this first before you tackle a long stretch of river. Or try going against the river current first so then you can turn around and just float back.

5 If you've conquered a single kayak, try a tandem kayak. It seems like tandem kayaking (two spots for people) would be easier, but this isn't the case. It's actually a lot harder because there are two people who are moving and rocking the kayak. You have to get used to each other and learn how to work together when using a tandem.

Jack's Top Tips and Takeaways

- **Wear a life jacket.** Not only is it a good idea to wear a life jacket, but it's also the law. You can get a ticket if you don't have one on.

- **Take a friend along.** It's good to go with someone when kayaking. This is because it helps to have someone help you flip the kayak back over if you happen to roll over.

- **Leave behind your valuables.** It doesn't take much for items like sunglasses or a phone to get lost in the lake. Even though you might be tempted to bring accessories along, just don't.

66

LEARN THREE DIFFERENT SWIM STROKES.

EVERYONE SHOULD MASTER SOME basic swim strokes at some point in their life. Not only will this keep you safe, it also makes being outside and in nature a lot more fun. There are so many great water sports to enjoy, so it's good to know how to swim. (But you should always wear your life jacket when doing these sports.) It's not just about being able to dog-paddle, though. It's also good to know some actual strokes.

1 Understand the different swim strokes. Some of the top ones include freestyle, breast, butterfly, backstroke, and sidestroke. Learn the correct way to do each of these before you attempt to do them on your own. You might even have someone watch you and give you feedback to make sure you're doing each one correctly. A lesson never hurts!

2 Practice in the pool, or another controlled location, to start. Work on each stroke a little at a time. If there's one that is particularly challenging, practice it even more. You'll be tired at first, but little by little you'll build up your strength in the water.

3 A lot of times, people will like swimming, but they don't really like going underwater. Don't let this be you. Part of being comfortable in the water is going under the water and not having to hold your nose. Practice this along with your swimming strokes so you feel really natural and comfortable in the water.

4 Now practice your swim strokes in a natural body of water. Once you really have the hang of your swim strokes and are good with going underwater, take your skills to a pond, river, or lake. Now do everything you practiced while getting used to water in an outdoor setting. The water might be warmer or colder. You might experience some ripples or small waves. You might find you want to wear water shoes because you don't like your feet touching the sandy, rocky bottom. All of these things are fine. You just have to get used to a new setting.

5 Finally, work on your overall speed and stamina. It won't take long before you're swimming more like a fish in the outdoors. You'll be diving into the water, showing off all your different swim strokes, and wanting to learn even more. Keep practicing your speed, and build up your endurance to be able to swim longer without getting tired.

Jack's Top Tips and Takeaways

- **Challenge your family or friends.** Create your own mini swim race with a friend where you have to swim back and forth in an area, changing swim strokes each time.

- **Keep kicking.** Don't forget to use your feet. You really have to make yourself get used to doing this over time. It will eventually start to feel natural.

- **Get it on video.** Sometimes it's hard to know if you have the right form. Have a friend or family member record you swimming so you can see what you're doing correctly and what you need to fix.

67
TRY WATERSKIING, KNEEBOARDING, OR TUBING.

IT'S TIME TO PUT YOUR ATHLETIC SKILLS to the test with some of these water sports. (Actually, you don't have to be very athletic at all to do tubing.) These are all great activities to try on a hot summer day. Or, if you're feeling really adventurous, do all the ones we've already discussed before crossing this one off your list!

1 Find someone with a motorboat. For these water sports, you need to go fast, so a speedboat is definitely a requirement. You'll also want to find a nice big open area for these sports. You want lots of room without it being supercrowded, especially if you're trying these activities for the first time. Be sure you go with someone who is an experienced boat driver, and don't forget your life jacket.

2 Learn the basics of tubing. The key to tubing is to hold on tight the entire time. When you first take off, there will definitely be a jerk or jolt that might catch you off guard. But after that, it's a pretty smooth ride. If you come across waves or bumps in the water, try to relax your body and just move with the movement instead of trying to brace yourself.

3 Practice your kneeboarding skills. Kneeboarding requires a special board that essentially helps you surf through the water on your knees. You'll want to work on your balance, leaning slightly back and keeping your elbows slightly bent as you're holding onto the rope. Again, it's important to try to stay relaxed. If you get too nervous, you might lock up and take a nosedive.

4 Now try to get up on skis. This is the toughest one to master! Skis can be big and bulky. You also start in the water in an awkward position, leaning back and with your skis sticking straight up into the air. As the boat starts to take off, you want to dig in almost like you're digging your heels into the water. Bend your knees slightly (but don't lock them) as you try to stand up in the water and zip across on your skis.

5 Now it's time to challenge yourself on one of these sports. If you've mastered one of these, then try to take it up a notch. For instance, if you're tubing, you might try going outside of the wake of the boat and then back to the middle, smooth area again. If you're kneeboarding or skiing, you might try to do a turn or slightly jump into the air.

Jack's Top Tips and Takeaways

- **Let it go.** If you feel yourself start to fall, it is OK to let go. As you're learning, it's part of the process to crash.

- **Try trainers.** If you have access to training skis, they're really great because they can help you keep the skis together in the water. It'll help you learn how to ski faster.

- **Be strong.** A lot of these sports require you to use your upper-body strength. Even if you don't think you have a lot of strength, hold on. You probably have more than you think. Just don't let go (unless you think you're going to crash . . . then see the first tip).

68
TRY SAILING.

SAILING HAS BEEN AROUND for so many years, and it's a big part of history. Experience this amazing outdoor hobby for yourself by hitting the waters and going out for a sail. It's unlike any boating experience you've ever had, and everyone should experience it at least once.

1 Become friends with someone who has a sailboat. This is an important first step. This way, they can teach you about sailing a little bit at a time. You could also sign up for a sailboat experience or rent one in your area or on vacation, but knowing someone directly is definitely a plus.

2 Learn some of the terms so you can talk the talk. What's the hull (it's below deck)? What's the mast (it holds up the sails)? Where's the bow (the front of the boat)? These are some of the basic sailing terms that would be good to learn if you're going to try this hobby for yourself. Ask questions and become familiar with the terms. This way you can communicate with other sailors as they are teaching you the basics.

3 Observe first before you try to step in and do everything. You might be tempted to jump in and take off, but this isn't the right hobby for that approach. Ask questions and be a good listener first and foremost. Sailing involves science and patience. You have to learn the right techniques and approach to have success at it.

4 Go out for a small sail, taking on some of the basic sailing duties. Listen to your captain and volunteer to be the first mate, taking orders and responding as the captain needs you. Start with a small trip, and then expand your duties a little at a time.

5 Now conquer a large sailing trip. After you gain some experience, challenge yourself to a longer sailing adventure. You should still work with someone who is an experienced sailor and can help you along the way instead of trying to do it all yourself. When you go out, breathe in the fresh air around you. There's something magical about traveling by wind.

Jack's Top Tips and Takeaways

- **Go for a ride.** Be a rider first before you start tackling some of the duties as a sailor. You can learn a lot about the terms and the process just by watching.

- **Watch it from afar.** Did you know sailboat races are a thing? Yep, they sure are. They can be really fun to watch, so go and find one in a coastal area.

- **Take it slow.** Sailing can be fast, but it's actually a more slow-paced sport. This is a good thing. This way, you are less likely to get seasick. Plus, you can enjoy your ride and look for fish and other wildlife.

⹀ 69 ⹀
GO WHITEWATER RAFTING.

THIS IS THE BIG ONE TO CONQUER in this chapter. It's a huge, challenging, tiring, and totally awesome water trip that you should have at least once growing up . . . or maybe even a few times. It's one of those adventure sports, so you might find you're hooked after one trip.

1 Find a good rafting guide to get started. They will help you find a place to go no matter what the time of year. They'll also be able to recommend when to go and different water options, based on your experience or comfort around the water.

2 Talk to your guide to help understand the rapids scaling system. This sport actually has a grading system so you can easily understand how difficult the rapids are. The levels are one through six, with one being the easiest and six being the toughest. You might be tempted to take on a challenge right away, but start small.

3 Get the proper training through your guide. Whitewater rafting is a thrill sport, which means it has some danger to it at the same time. Be sure that you go through all the training required before it's time to get on the river. Yes, you should wear a life jacket at all times. And you should absolutely know what to do in case of an emergency or if someone in the raft goes overboard. One of the basics is knowing that if you fall overboard, you should get to the shore as quickly as possible instead of staying in the center of the river, so you don't get swept away. Go through the entire training before you ever get out on the water.

4 Get started with lots of practice. This will likely mean a class-1 or class-2 stream, and going over lots of little bumps or fast areas. This is a good thing! As you go, you'll really start to read the river, and you can apply this knowledge on a bigger or more rapid whitewater area.

5 Now go on a more challenging whitewater adventure—but still stick with a guide. It can be a longer trip or a higher level. Ask your guide for a recommendation, and let her help you increase your skills as you go. Then you'll be able to build your skills to conquer more and more rivers in your future.

Jack's Top Tips and Takeaways

- **Go somewhere cool.** It's fun to find a destination rafting trip, and there are plenty of options out there to choose from. There are lots of opinions on the best options, but both Glacier National Park and the Grand Canyon are high on my list.

- **Check the number of people.** If it's your first time rafting and you're going out with twelve to fifteen people, this might not be the best experience. It might be better to start with a smaller group so you can get good experience and gain confidence.

MOUNTAINEERING

"THE MOUNTAINS ARE CALLING, AND I MUST GO."

—JOHN MUIR

Mountains are some of the most enormous and impressive sights in nature. They stand so tall in the distance, and on clear days you can see their peaks peeking up into the skyline from miles and miles away.

John Muir was right that mountains seem to call people, luring them in closer and closer. It's really not enough to just see a mountain in the distance. You need to experience it for yourself. From the fresh mountain air to the amazing animals you could find, it's time to go and start checking things off your list.

≋ 70 ≋
SPOT A MOUNTAIN ANIMAL.

ONE OF THE BIGGEST DRAWS to mountains for many people is the opportunity to see cool or unique animals. Bears, moose, elk, and mountain goats are just a few of the animals that people look for in mountains each year. Ready to make your mountain trip really special?

1 Learn what animals you can see on the mountains you plan to visit. This will vary a great deal based on location, but it's easy to find with a quick Google search. Or, if you're using a guidebook for the area, it'll likely have tips of what to look for. Set a goal of the top five to seven animals you're hoping to see, and then try to spot at least three of them.

2 Stop at the visitor center in a nearby town. The park rangers and visitor center workers likely have the best and latest information about what people are seeing in the park or mountains. They're also happy and willing to share this information, so it's definitely worth a stop. You can learn locations, best time of day, and other good information to increase your chances of seeing a mountain animal.

3 Start out early in the morning. Sunrise is always a good time for animals to be on the move. This will require you to get up early (probably even before sunrise), but it can really pay off. Plus, you'll get a great mountain view.

4 Go quietly. It's so easy to spook animals as you're clomping through the forests and up the mountain trails. Try to move swiftly and quietly. This will also allow you to listen for signs of animals in the distance.

5 When you spot an animal, give it space and observe its behavior. You don't want to creep up on it and scare it or make it feel threatened. Remember, it's a wild animal, and it can hurt you.

Jack's Top Tips and Takeaways

- **Try the evening.** Early morning is definitely a prime viewing time, but you can also try going at dusk. This will let you see animals that are about to go in for the night or nocturnal animals about to come out.

- **Bring your binoculars.** Binoculars aren't just for bird watching. You can also use them to find wild animals in the distance. Even if the animals are large, it helps to use binoculars to be able to pick them out and zoom in on their details.

- **Focus around water areas.** Every animal needs water, so this is a good place to go to spot them. They will have to go to the water area at some point. So if you're patient enough, there's a good chance you'll see a cool wild animal eventually.

71

PAN FOR GOLD.

HAVE YOU EVER HEARD THE PHRASE, "There's gold in them thar hills." It's definitely an old saying and doesn't have the best grammar, but there is some truth in it. A common place to find gold is in mountainous areas, so try panning for mountain gold at least once before you grow up.

1 Learn about gold panning. While gold panning is more of a hobby than an opportunity to get rich, it's still a lot of fun. Mountain streams are great places to pan for gold because of gravity. The water brings down erosion and materials from high in the mountains. Where the river or stream starts to slow is a good place to pan because materials will often settle there.

2 Find a place to go. This might require a little bit (or a lot) of traveling if you don't have good panning opportunities near you. If you happen to be already planning a vacation, just do some searching to see if there are nearby mountains known for having gold.

3 Sign up for some panning lessons. It's not difficult, but you do have to learn what to look for, the right equipment to use, and how to sift through the rocks and sand in the right way so you don't miss any gold. You also have to know how to spot fool's gold (pyrite), which isn't real gold. It tends to be shiny or brassy while real gold is more yellow in tone. Find a place that has group panning lessons and pull in a few friends to join you. The instructor will show you the ropes and get you ready to try it on your own.

4 After you've learned the basics, you're ready to try it on your own. There's something magical about the thought of finding gold in a totally remote area in a mountain stream. You know you're probably not going to get rich, but it doesn't stop you from chasing the dream!

5 Don't forget to look for other unique opportunities outside of gold panning. There are areas throughout the country where you can look for precious gemstones, like emeralds, rubies, or diamonds. You might also just want to be on the lookout for areas with cool or rare rocks. Now, it can be illegal to collect rocks in certain areas (like national parks or some public beaches), so abide by the laws in the area.

Jack's Top Tips and Takeaways

- **Head to Alaska.** This is one of the most epic places to go panning for gold because a lot of the land is wild, untouched, and unexplored. It gives you the thrill of discovering something amazing.

- **Collect the pieces.** You might only find little flecks of gold, but you can put these together in a tiny little tube for a cool necklace or piece of jewelry.

72

SUMMIT A MOUNTAIN.

YOU CAN'T BEAT THE VIEW FROM ON TOP of a mountain, especially on a clear day. This is why so many people love mountains and chase after that picture-perfect view from the very top. It's not an easy task to accomplish, though. You better grab those hiking shoes.

1 Find a mountain you want to get all the way to the top of. There are opportunities to summit a big hill or mountain pretty much anywhere you go. You'll find big and small mountains available in nearly every state, so there are plenty of options to choose from.

2 Know your limits. There are some pretty amazing, epic, and even dangerous mountains out there. Some people die trying to reach the top of mountains each year, which involves more serious climbing. It can be incredibly difficult, especially when you start dealing with mountains that have snow and ice at the top, not to mention the rise in altitude that makes it so much harder to breathe. Start with a small, manageable goal to summit a mountain.

3 Start a training plan. Even if you're tackling a smaller mountain, you need a training plan. Activities like hiking, stair climbing, and running can increase your overall endurance and get you ready for your big day. Definitely hike hills and rough terrain as part of your training to get you ready for similar trails.

4 Pick the right time of year to go, and start planning. Bad weather during a hike to summit a mountain can make your experience miserable or even dangerous. Don't do it. It really makes a difference when you've planned ahead to find the right time of year and day to go. If you have bad weather one day, don't be afraid to postpone the trip.

5 Breathe in that mountain air at the top, and take in that amazing view. Getting to the top is such an incredible feeling, and you should enjoy the moment. Sit down. Look at the amazing view. Snap a few pictures so you can remember it later. You're not done yet . . . you still have to go down, which some people say is more challenging than going up. But you just accomplished a huge goal, and it's something to celebrate.

Jack's Top Tips and Takeaways

- **Pack water and snacks.** Just like hiking, make sure you bring lots of good water. You can get one of those backpacks with a water pouch in it so you don't have to carry heavy bottles. A few healthy, calorie-dense snacks can help you restore your energy levels for the hike down.

- **Dress in layers.** It can be a lot colder as you go toward the top of the mountain. So you might start with short sleeves and then add on layers as you go.

- **Wear good shoes.** Hiking up a mountain can include a lot of uneven surfaces. Be sure you have good shoes with good tread on the bottom.

⟩ 73 ⟨

CAPTURE AN AMAZING VIEW ON CAMERA.

YOU DON'T HAVE TO SUMMIT a mountain to capture a great view. In fact, some of the best mountain views are not at the very top. For this goal, you want to find good scenic opportunities or lookout points that will give you that Instagram-worthy pic.

1 Look for the lookout opportunities. Every popular mountain area will likely have scenic pullouts and overlooks that you can drive to. Some of the really great viewpoints will require some hiking, too, but these will likely be marked on a map.

2 Do some photo research on your own. If you do an image search on Google or Instagram of the mountain area you're in, then you'll start seeing images from this area. (Search social media sites using hashtags. For instance, if you're visiting a national park, search #Yosemite to see where other people are going.) With the sites that have recent photos, take a look at where these images were specifically taken from. Do you like a certain scene more than another? Find out where it was taken, and then go there.

3 Now look for those hidden or secret spots that only the locals know about. It's easy to find the places that everyone knows

about, but now seek out the ones that are off the beaten path. Go to local visitor centers or ask around at local shops. If you're nice and friendly, the locals just might be willing to reveal some of those hidden gems.

4 Set yourself up for the perfect shot. How do you do this? No, it's not about having the perfect tripod or fancy camera. You just need to be at the right place at the right time. Maybe you snap an amazing picture during the height of fall color. Or perhaps you get an amazing sunset off into the horizon. Capturing a moment like this just takes a little planning . . . knowing when to go—both time of day and time of year—is huge.

5 Now that you snapped that perfect picture, what will you do with it? Don't just post it to social media. Turn it into an art or poster print to hang in your room. Print a set of postcards and send them out to friends. Enter it into a local photo contest. Then keep finding those great views and taking more great pictures.

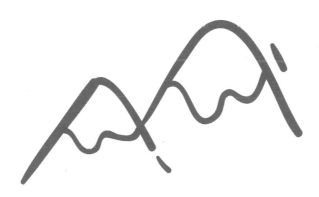

Jack's Top Tips and Takeaways

- **Try different angles.** Sometimes just a slightly different angle can make a huge difference in the subject of the photograph. Try different points of view to get that perfect shot.

- **Go to the water.** Water surfaces like lakes and rivers always make for a good picture opportunity. Frame up your photo (and try those different angles) with water in it, and try to capture the reflection of the mountain in the water.

- **Go at sunset.** A few minutes can sometimes change everything. For instance, a sunset happens over 20 to 30 minutes, and the lighting changes with every moment. (Movie directors call this the Magic Hour.) One time, I was taking a photo of the sunset, and just 2 minutes later, the sky turned a beautiful pink and purple. It made for a much better photo.

74
GO ROCK CLIMBING.

ROCK CLIMBING IS DEFINITELY A SPORT for people who like a thrill. If you've ever done indoor rock climbing, you know how difficult and tiring it can be. So now you're just taking it outside. Yeah, there's no "just" in this one. Get ready to be challenged!

1 Practice inside first . . . a lot. Inside rock climbing is so much fun, and it's great practice to get you ready for your first outdoor experience. Definitely take a class at a local gym where a seasoned instructor can teach you the ropes. You'll learn the basics of the harness system and how to climb safely. It's really important to learn all these things and put them into practice as you go.

2 In addition to training inside at a climbing gym, you want to really work on your upper-body strength. You'll need it to help pull yourself up from one area to the next. Push-ups are a simple (and really effective) way to build up this strength.

3 Take it outside . . . with a guide. No matter how much you climb inside, it's just different when you take it outdoors. Hire someone who is trained and experienced and who can help you transfer your knowledge and skills. A guide will know a good place for beginners and make sure you are being completely safe.

4 Conquer a small goal first. Let your guide lead you on this one. You might be tempted to go bigger, but climbing outside adds a whole new layer of difficulty.

5 Go bigger a little at a time. You don't want to overdo it on this one. People die every year from rock climbing, usually because they aren't being safe or properly secured. Do not try to go without safety precautions or go too big too fast. This adventure is one in which you want to build up your skills slowly. Many experienced rock climbers have been practicing their entire lives.

Jack's Top Tips and Takeaways

- **Find a place to go regularly.** You can often get a good deal on seasonal climbing passes at indoor gyms, making it more affordable to go regularly. See if they have a youth climbing club—an added bonus where you can invite your friends to join you. And, yes, this really is a thing. It's a good way to learn technique and even become competitive.

- **Try wearing gloves.** Even though you might not think you need gloves, it might be good to wear them. Gloves will help you avoid blisters and get a good grip when you're climbing. The staff at the gym can point you in the direction of where to buy the proper gear.

BEACHING

"I COULD NEVER STAY LONG ENOUGH ON THE SHORE; THE TANG OF THE UNTAINTED, FRESH, AND FREE SEA AIR WAS LIKE A COOL, QUIETING THOUGHT."

—HELEN KELLER

Water is one of the most soothing sounds of nature, making beaches some of the most popular destinations around the world. From gentle tides to crashing waves, beaches attract millions of visitors each year. And it's not hard to understand why.

Beaches are filled with life. You can always find birds flying about, insects scurrying along the edges of the water, and plenty of sea creatures both in and out of the water. Here are some of the best things you can do at the beach to really experience nature to the fullest.

75

EXPLORE THE TIDE POOLS.

TIDE POOLS OFFER A GLIMPSE into ocean life that you wouldn't otherwise be able to see. Just a peek down into a tide pool will often reveal all sorts of cool animals and sea creatures. You might see these animals in a zoo or aquarium, but now is your chance to see them in real life.

1 Know where to go. Tide pools are essentially holes within the ground where you can find anemones, sea stars, sea urchins, and other ocean life. Not all beaches have tide pool areas. You need to go to a spot where the tide comes in and out each day. You also want to look for an area where there are big and sturdy rocks you can walk across to get to the tide pools. If you're unsure, ask around for a good suggestion.

2 Check the tide schedule. You can find high and low tide charts for any beach town online, just like you can find the sunrise and sunset time. You can probably even put your question into Google, and it'll give you the answer based on where you're located. If you're going to a specific beach, plan to show up about an hour ahead of the low tide time.

3 Wear good shoes. You're often walking around slippery underwater rocks. It's important to be careful because it's so easy to slip and fall. Try to wear shoes with a good grip—or shoes specifically made for the water ("water shoes")—to help you as you navigate across rocks to explore the tide pools.

4 Try to identify what you see. The coolest thing about tide pools is seeing animals that you had no idea were animals due to their stillness in the water or the shells they hide in. It helps to go with someone who knows what to look for. You can also find a guide or pictures (sometimes even at a local visitor center or park) to help you know what to look for. As you gaze down into the tide

pool, try to identify different creatures. Don't touch them at all, but definitely admire them from a distance.

5 Don't get caught up in the tide as it comes back. It's easy to get engrossed up in looking in the tide pools, but as the tide rises the water will slowly fill back into the area. Don't let yourself get stranded. Do your looking and then get out of there. You can always come back the next day.

Jack's Top Tips and Takeaways

- **Look on the side.** Don't forget to look on the sides of tide pools, not just directly down. Fascinating creatures, like starfish, tend to cling to the sides.

- **Try to find an anemone.** Remember where Nemo lived in the movie *Finding Nemo*? That is a sea anemone. It looks like a plant, but did you know it's also half animal? You can often find them in tide pools.

- **Get a closer look.** Use a magnifying glass to help you look for details and pick out animals in the tide pool.

⋛ 76 ⋚
LOOK FOR WHALES OR DOLPHINS.

WHEN YOU'RE LOOKING OUT AT THE OCEAN and see a whale or a dolphin jump from the water in the distance, it's truly one of the coolest animal sightings you can have. It's not always an easy thing to accomplish, but you can help achieve this goal with a few tricks.

1 Know where to look. First off, you have to know if you're going to a beach area that even has whale and dolphin sightings. If seeing these animals is on your list of things you really want to do, you might want to plan a trip around places known for these types of sightings. Then you can research the best beaches to visit in that area.

2 Ask the locals. They will definitely know where to look and can get you pointed in the right direction. Ask around at local visitor centers, bait shops, and even little stores or restaurants near the beach. If they don't know exactly where to tell you to go, they can likely tell you who to ask.

3 Take along binoculars. Scanning for these animals while you're on the shore can be difficult. It's so easy for a wave or even a bird to look like something jumping from the water. By having binoculars, you can do a quick scan off into the distance. Do a Google image search of "dolphin (or whale) jumping in the ocean," which will help you get a general idea of the shape you're trying to find.

4 If you're not having luck on the beach but you really want to accomplish this goal, consider signing up for a dolphin- or whale-watching tour. The captains of these tour boats know where to go, and the tours are designed to maximize the chances of a sighting. If it's a good day, you're almost guaranteed to have a sighting—and often more than just one.

5 For a challenge, try to see both whales and dolphins in a single day. This isn't going to be an easy task, but it will be epic. You will increase your chances of accomplishing this one by having access to a boat—and perhaps the above-mentioned sightseeing tour. Starting early in the morning will also help.

Jack's Top Tips and Takeaways

- **Always be on the lookout.** You never know when you might have an epic whale or dolphin sighting. Beyond specifically looking for them, any time you're around the ocean is a good time to keep your eyes peeled and on the waves. You never know when you might see a fin cutting through the water.

- **Take along meds.** If you're going to go out on a whale-watching boat, you might want to take some medicine so you don't get seasick. This could ruin your trip, and you don't want to do that.

- **Look for a chance to swim with the dolphins.** There are some really cool opportunities to swim with the dolphins. You may not find this naturally in the wild, however. Often, you can have this experience at aquariums or other centers that house such animals. These dolphins usually have been rescued in some way. Florida and California both have opportunities like this. So if it's high on your list, go check it out.

⋛ 77 ⋜
SEARCH FOR SEA GLASS.

SHELLS AREN'T THE ONLY THINGS TO LOOK for as you're walking along the beach. You'll also want to keep an eye out for bright and shiny beach glass in the sand. With many shades like green, blue, and pink, you have so much to find. Start searching!

1 Learn what sea glass is. Sea glass is little pieces of glass that have broken off and been rolled around by the sea, making them smooth, bright, and beautiful. While the glass can come from almost anything, the history of sea glass dates from glass from old shipwrecks. Sea glass can often roll around in the ocean for decades or even hundreds of years before it ends up on the shore. By then, the glass definitely has smoothed out and looks like rock.

2 Find the best beaches for sea glass. Any beach can have sea glass, but some are more known for it than others. If you're traveling to the beach, do a Google search or ask around for the best places to find sea glass. Some colors are rarer than others (like the really bright blues), so knowing good places to go will increase your chances of finding nice or rare pieces.

3 Challenge yourself to find sea glass in four or five different shades. You can easily find sea glass in light pinks or even white colors. Then you'll likely find greens, as well. Try to find several different colors of sea glass. Even different shades of a green or a blue can count.

4 Collect enough sea glass to fill a cup. Sea glass pieces are often small, so it's not easy to fill a cup. If you're with a friend, each of you should have the same size cup and then see who can fill it first. It'll help make this adventure more challenging.

5 Make something cool out of your sea glass. Now that you have all these pieces in various colors, turn it into something cool. You can make a mosaic out of it. You could put all the pieces in a little jar. You could write out your name or initials with the pieces. No matter what you decide to do, display your sea glass proudly because you did all the work of finding it. Plus, it's beautiful.

Jack's Top Tips and Takeaways

- **Stop and dig.** Digging can be a great way to unearth some sea glass. So stay in one spot instead of just walking along the beach. Just be sure to return the sand to fill any divets you created during your dig.

- **Wear protective shoes.** If you're on a rocky beach (which can be really good for finding sea glass), don't forget to wear good water shoes with sturdy soles.

- **Go off the beaten path.** Don't just go in the path where everyone else is walking. Change it up to go in areas that don't have a lot of traffic. This way, you'll see spots that others haven't.

78

HELP WITH A BEACH CLEANUP.

OUR BEACHES NEED US! Beaches across the country are being filled with plastic, trash, and other litter. It's very rewarding to be part of a cleanup effort. It makes you realize just how important it is to keep our beaches clean.

1 Find a beach that's important to you. Any beach will do, but it always seems to make a bigger difference when you have a tie to it in some way. Do you have a beach that you love? Or maybe it's one you like to visit when you're on vacation. Either way, find a beach that you really want to help improve and be part of a cleanup.

2 If you can't find a cleanup effort already scheduled, start your own. While it can be really awesome to join a big cleanup effort (you can really see the results quickly), you don't have to go this route. Every little bit helps, so start your own event, and spread the word.

3 Now it's time to bring in family, friends, and neighbors to help with the beach cleanup. Set a date and time. You might even do a sign-up for people to bring snacks, water, garbage bags, and more. Try to get a lot of people involved, and you'll see just how much you can accomplish in an hour or two.

4 Get out and start cleaning. When it's cleaning day, be sure you have enough garbage bags and gloves to go around. It's nice for everyone to have a bag (or put people into teams), and then challenge them to fill the bag. To get even more accomplished, divide up the areas and assign people to certain sections. This is where it really helps to divide and conquer.

5 Celebrate at the end. Doing a beach cleanup is hard, messy work. At the end of the day, you'll be tired. Be sure to celebrate your accomplishments by doing something to enjoy the beach. Then in the future when you're enjoying the beach, be sure to clean up after yourself so someone else doesn't have to.

Jack's Top Tips and Takeaways

- **Make it an official event.** Ask your parents to create an event on Facebook to host your own beach cleanup. It's a great way to spread the word and invite others.

- **Turn it into a project.** A lot of times, you have an opportunity to do a community or service project through your class or school. Make a beach cleanup one of these projects.

- **Take pictures.** Before and after pictures can really help show the impact you made in just a few hours. Show them to everyone who was there so they know how much their efforts really mattered.

79

GO SHELLING.

ONE OF THE MOST POPULAR ACTIVITIES at the beach is to look for seashells in the sand. As you walk along the shore, you hope to find something unique, rare, or just really beautiful. Here are some tips for going shelling during your next beach outing.

1 Look for shells during low tide. This is one of the best times to look because the tide will wash them in and out. So it gives you the chance to see and find shells coming on shore for the first time, or to see shells that were covered by water before. Low tide will allow you to get closer to the ocean. Just make sure you get out of there before the tide starts to rise again.

2 Get out on a full moon. The tide is known for being more rapid and active during full moons. This means the ocean is more forceful, bringing in more shells from the ocean or washing away sand from the shore. Plus, wouldn't it be cool to look for shells in the early evening during a full moon?

3 Go off the beaten path. If you want to find the really unusual or unique shells, then you need to go where other people aren't looking. Go exploring at the side beaches instead of the main ones. You could also go early in the morning when fewer people are out looking. Both tricks will increase your chances of being able to find cool shells.

4 Seek out those really amazing, epic beaches. Some of the best beaches for finding shells are in the Gulf Shores. But even then, it helps to know which ones to go to. Even if you're not in this area but are on vacation, do some research to find the best beach in that area to find shells.

5 Try to collect all different shells. Yes, there are different types and styles of shells. A good online guide to check out is the Florida website, www.2fla.com/Florida_Shells. From cockle to conch shells, this site will help you learn all the different shell options and start checking them off your list!

Jack's Top Tips and Takeaways

- **Turn it into a game.** Now that you know different shell types, choose four different types of shells you want to find. Then go with a friend and see who can find them first and in the best condition.

- **Go along the edges.** If you wade along the edge of the water, you might also see some cool shells to dig up or ones being washed ashore.

- **Do a craft with shells.** Look for ways to display your shells. You might put them along the bottom of a glass jar where you have a plant. Or you could glue them around a picture frame and put your favorite picture from the beach in the middle.

80
SKIP A ROCK AT LEAST TEN TIMES.

EVERYONE SHOULD LEARN GOOD rock-skipping technique at some point. This is a hobby and skill you can put into practice at any water area, including lakes, ponds, streams, and, of course, at the beach. Now, skipping a rock once or twice is easy enough, but making it to ten times is not easy. Here are a few tips.

1 Find the right rock shape. There are a lot of different opinions about the right type of rock for skipping. We recommend finding a rock that is a bit triangular in shape with pointed, yet slightly smooth, edges. This will allow you to hold it easily between your thumb and forefinger, which is the perfect way to skip a rock.

2 Find the right rock size. This will vary a lot from one person to the next, but overall, you don't want it to be too big to handle. This includes how big it is and how heavy it is. You mostly have to test this out for yourself to find your perfect kind of rock. So start picking up rocks and tossing them. You'll quickly figure out what works for you.

3 Get low to the water. The lower you can get to the water, the better. You want the rock to just float above the water before the first bounce so it will continue to go up higher and higher. If you start too high, then the rock will just go down into the water instead of bouncing across it.

4 Try a side-arm angle. If you throw your rock like a baseball, it'll go downward directly into the water. Instead, you want to throw it on the side, almost parallel to the water's surface, so the rock goes across the water. Extend your arm back far and flick your elbow area and wrist. It's similar to hitting a tennis ball with a racket, except it's even lower.

5 Keep practicing. Ten skips is no easy task. You're going to have to work on this one a lot before you master it. You might want to give up, but don't do it. If you have trouble getting ten skips, you might try to look for really calm water, like a lake or a pond, instead of bumpy water with lots of waves.

Jack's Top Tips and Takeaways

- **Get in the water.** You can stay on the shore to skip rocks, but if the water is nice enough, don't be afraid to get in there, at least waist deep. This will allow you to get close to the water, giving you a different angle for good skipping.

- **Look for calm waters.** Your rocks will skip better if the water is smooth. Lots of waves will get in the way of the bounces. Early mornings tend to yield more peaceful waters, so try skipping rocks in the morning.

- **Gather up several rocks at a time.** When you're in the mindset of looking for a good rock, you want to keep hunting to find good options. So pile several together at once before you practice your skipping. It'll give you lots to work with, too!

WINTERING

"YOU CAN'T GET TOO MUCH WINTER IN THE WINTER."

—ROBERT FROST

Don't be one of those people who just stay inside during winter. This season tends to get a bad reputation, but it is filled with great outdoor adventure opportunities. You just have to have the right clothing and gear. Then it can be just as fun and busy as any other season.

Here are some of the top activities you can conquer during winter. If you want to be really ambitious, see how many of these you can get to in a single season. It's definitely possible to hit them all!

81

GO SNOWSHOEING.

THIS IS ONE OF THE EASIEST WINTER SPORTS to conquer. Yes, you might need some special shoes, but that's about it. Once you have them on, you can really just get up and start walking. Oh, and it'll help if you have some snow, too.

1 Learn what type of snowshoes you need. Snowshoes are broken up into three categories depending on the terrain you'll be on: flat, rolling, and mountain terrain. Most people and places fall into the category of flat terrain. This is usually a basic snowshoe that is good for your backyard, neighborhood, and most area parks. If you have the chance, definitely try on snowshoes before you buy them so you know what feels comfortable. You strap snowshoes onto your own shoe or boot, but you still want to test them out for weight and overall comfort.

2 Find snow to test out your shoes. You might have to travel a bit to find a good area for snowshoes. Or perhaps this is something you're trying on vacation instead. (If you're on vacation near a mountain resort, you can often rent snowshoes and test them on the spot.) If you have the opportunity, try to snowshoe in freshly fallen snow. It might make it a little more difficult to walk because the snow is not packed in yet, but it's really cool to make the first set of tracks in a snowy yard or field.

3 If you're going up a hill and you're on powdery snow, try stepping and then kicking out to help make your tracks and pack in the snow. If it's already packed in, be careful going uphill because the surface could be slick. You might want to have poles to help you get a good grip, and then you want to use the best traction area of your snowshoes to bite into the snow.

4 For going downhill, poles definitely help you keep your balance. Since your weight wants to move forward, practice setting your weight back a little bit, which likely means you'll have to sink back in your heels. You don't want your weight to move forward too much because you could topple over, especially if you hit a slick patch.

5 Now try running in your snowshoes. You probably shouldn't do this one while going uphill or downhill, but it's an awesome skill to master. It's not going to be easy, though. You'll want to work your way up to this gradually, from a walk to a small jog to finally a run. Try recruiting a friend to have a snowshoe race.

Jack's Top Tips and Takeaways

- **Ask to borrow.** Try borrowing snowshoes first so you can test different ones out before buying your own. Ask around to your family or friends to see who might know someone with snowshoes you can try. If you're at a mountain resort, oftentimes they'll have snowshoes for rent.

- **Use your imagination.** If you're learning to snowshoe for the first time, think about making your steps big like a giant. Since the snowshoes make your feet a lot bigger and kind of clunky, you don't want to step on yourself over and over again.

- **Look for a trail.** If you're having a tough time getting the hang of snowshoes, try to find a trail or area that has already been packed down by others. This will help give you a sturdy foundation.

= 82 =
TRY CROSS-COUNTRY SKIING.

AFTER YOU GRADUATE FROM SNOWSHOES, the next step is cross-country skis. They are a bit more challenging than snowshoes, but it's another hobby that just about anyone can do. Just strap your boots on and take off.

1 Find the right skis. There are three main types, including performance, backcountry, and traditional. For the purpose of trying cross-country skiing for the first time, focus on traditional. Most ski sizes are listed in centimeters. You'll want to figure out your height in centimeters and then add 25 centimeters. Keep in mind that you might adjust based on your size or weight, but it's a good start. Poles are most often based on height, but you will want to cross-check to see what's comfortable.

2 Practice the motion of cross-country skiing. Have you ever been on an elliptical machine? It's different from a treadmill because it's more of a smooth, continuous motion, between a walk and a run. This is how you should look while cross-country skiing. With each step of your leg, the opposite arm moves forward with your pole. This motion continues, rotating back and forth.

3 Start on a groomed trail. Look for a cross-country skiing trail system near you because it will have groomed trails that are easier for first-time skiers. Most of the time, these trails already have tracks packed down, so it makes it a smooth ride for you.

4 Now go off the beaten path to make your own trail. This is a lot more challenging, but it's fun to go off trail to make your own path instead. This is more like backcountry skiing. You don't need to switch to a different ski. Just know that you should take it slow as you're making your own path, and start on fairly flat surfaces.

5 Tackle challenges to ski like a pro. If you fall, can you get back up? Can you go both uphill and downhill easily? Can you increase and decrease your speed? As you get more comfortable on your skis, tackle all of these. If you can accomplish each one, you'll know you're ready for even more challenging trails.

Jack's Top Tips and Takeaways

- **Buy used.** You can rent skis, but another option is to buy used. Sports stores will often have a second-hand section or a ski swap from seasons past. You can get great deals, and then use those skis all season instead of renting over and over again.

- **Try on lots of boots.** Along with skis, you'll need cross-country boots that clip in and attach to the skis. This is often more important to get right than the skis. Try on lots of different options to make sure you get one that is comfortable for you.

- **Pick up speed.** After you've gotten the hang of cross-country skiing by going on trails, try picking up speed on a hill by bending your knees and leaning slightly forward.

83
TRY DOWNHILL SKIING.

MANY PEOPLE WHO TRY downhill skiing love it, and then they are skiers for life. In fact, they can't wait for winter to roll back around so they can go skiing again. It takes a little effort to find the right place to go and to gather the right equipment, but it's worth it.

1 Find a place to go. This is one hobby that you can't just do anywhere. You need a ski hill to go down, so you have to do a little research to find one in your area. If you don't live in a particularly snowy area, you might have to drive a ways or travel. If it's not a very snowy year, don't worry. Those ski hill areas often make their own snow during the winter. Just call ahead to make sure they have good ski conditions.

2 Rent equipment. Skiing can be expensive, so if you're just trying it out for the first time, don't worry about buying everything you need. Just rent it instead. A lot of times, the ski resorts and areas will have this as an option. If you're not sure, call first. Otherwise, check out your local outdoors store and ask if they rent ski equipment instead. This way you can go in and try things on first.

3 Take a lesson. If you've never done downhill skiing, it's best to sign up for a lesson. The insructor will help you learn the essentials and test out your skis to get you off on the right foot. You might look at someone downhill skiing and think you can easily pull it off on your own, but don't make this mistake. A ski instructor is definitely the way to go for the first time.

4 Hit the slopes. You want to start off small. This is usually called the bunny slope, and you might not want to go on it because this is where all the little kids start. But this will help you build up your balance, confidence, and skills.

5 Increase your difficulty a little at a time. Even though you need to start on a bunny slope, it doesn't mean you have to stay there for very long. As you gain experience and knowledge about skiing, keep challenging yourself. You don't want to graduate from one slope to the next too quickly, but set yourself a goal in a single season, and then set out to achieve it.

Jack's Top Tips and Takeaways

- **Research lesson options.** You'll likely pay a small fee, but it's worth it to get you started. Just call ahead and ask for times and rates at different locations. This might help you decide where to go.

- **Stay relaxed.** You know how you need to keep your knees loose for paddleboarding? You don't want to lock them up at all. This is similar with skiing. Stay relaxed and ready to adjust at all times.

- **Don't try to go too fast too soon.** You will probably think about wanting to go fast on downhill skis right away because that's what you see in videos. Don't try to do this. Just stay nice and slow until you gain confidence and skills.

≥ 84 ≤
GO ICE FISHING.

IF YOU LOVE FISHING but tend to put your pole in storage after fall, then it's time to get it back out. Everyone should try ice fishing at some point. This winter sport is a good way to keep fishing year-round, and it's really not as cold as you might think.

1 Find an experienced ice fisherman to go with. This is an important one. Ice fishing can be dangerous if you don't know what you're doing. The ice needs to be thick enough for you to sit on, and an experienced person will know how to read this and properly prep the ice. If it doesn't get cold enough to ice fish in your area, then put this on your travel list to tackle during a winter trip.

2 Check your equipment. For basic ice fishing, you'll need a chisel, skimmer, pole, bait, and something to sit on. Of course, if you find someone with experience to go with, he'll likely have many of these things. If you get lucky, he'll even have a little ice shanty to go into, which will help keep you warm.

3 Bundle up. Ice fishing doesn't have to be a cold, chilling sport. You just need to dress properly. Be sure to wear layers, and if you have coveralls or overalls, that's a plus, too. You'll also want to wear thick wool socks, a hat, and gloves. If you happen to have gloves that can lift halfway off, this is awesome. This way your fingers can still work the process of fishing (like baiting the hook) without completely taking the gloves off.

4 Put your line in and wait. Ice fishing will likely test your patience. This is because it can involve a lot of waiting until you get a bite. Most ice fishermen will use a bobber of some sort. Then they'll put their line in and wait.

5 Start reeling! As soon as you see that bobber go down, it's time to hook your fish. Pay attention because that initial jerk on the line can make all the difference.

Jack's Top Tips and Takeaways

- **Don't forget the most important supply.** Yes, you need all the right fishing equipment, but one of the most important other items you can bring is a thermos of hot chocolate. When it's cold out, you'll be so glad you have this.

- **Change your fishing line.** You can often use a regular fishing pole for ice fishing instead of getting special equipment, but you might need to use a heavier fishing string. Ask someone who does ice fishing regularly to check your line.

- **Take along some entertainment.** It can definitely get boring waiting for the fish to bite. I like to bring along cards or a cribbage board so I have something to do while I wait.

≡ 85 ≡
MAKE A SNOW FORT.

ANY TIME OF YEAR IS A GOOD TIME to build a fort, but making one in winter is especially fun—and challenging at the same time. Get a good pair of gloves ready because it could take several hours to build a strong fort for winter.

1 Smooth out an area for your fort. Your fort is only as strong as the base. If you're building a fort on top of existing snow, then you'll want to get out a snow shovel and dig down to the bare ground. Or at least do what you can to make the bottom level and secure.

2 Make and create snow bricks. You can find brick-making shapes and supplies in the store or online, but you can also just improvise. If you have plastic tupperware or even bread pans in a rectangle shape, these are perfect. Pack your snow in tight, and then dump it out to create the brick, much like you'd do with a sand castle.

3 As you complete your bricks, you'll want to start stacking them along the outline of your snow fort. You might try offsetting each layer slightly so the seams to the snow blocks don't all line up. This will help your fort be more secure.

4 Add water to make it more solid. You don't want to overdo it with the water, but adding it a little bit at a time can really help your fort walls. Some people will wait until the end to do this, but we like to do it as we go. Drizzling water over each layer will turn those bricks into partial ice to make them really sturdy.

5 Add lights and other fort decorations. Once you have your fort built, decorate it. A flag would be perfect coming out of the top. Or you could get LED lights that don't require a plug-in. (This looks really cool at night, too.)

Jack's Top Tips and Takeaways

- **Don't overdo it.** Giant forts are awesome, but they are also a *lot* of work. Try not to be overly ambitious in trying to create a giant fort because this can take a lot of blocks. Instead, think smaller at first, and then you can always add on if you want.

- **Get help.** It takes a lot of time to create all the blocks you need for a fort. This is a perfect reason to invite family and friends over for a fort-building party. Seriously, the more the merrier.

- **Be smart with your positioning.** If you want to save on some work, position your fort against a wall so you only have to build three walls. You will be so glad you did this!

86

GO SLEDDING.

SLEDDING IS ONE OF THE GREATEST winter activities ever. You don't need to be experienced or have a lot of equipment to go sledding. It's really an activity that any age can do. So gather up all your family and friends to make the most of a good winter sledding day.

1 Find the best sledding hills in your area. The best sledding spots will have both big and small hills for a wide range of ages and skills. If you don't know of a good sledding spot where you live, just do a Google search or ask around at a local outdoors store or nature center. They'll be able to tell you where to go. Or do the same if you're in a new-to-you spot.

2 Dress for success. You will likely get wet, soggy, and messy when sledding. Be sure to wear good socks, boots, and layers to keep you warm. Also, don't forget mittens, hats, and scarves.

3 Go over the safety precautions. Sledding can be a dangerous sport, especially if there are trees around. Even if there aren't trees, you might want to be cautious and wear a helmet (bike helmets work great). You might want to practice steering the sled—lean in the direction you want to go. And, finally, if you feel like you're starting to lose control, know how to bail to avoid a crash. This is easy. You just roll off the side and let your sled go.

4 Hit the hills. When you're bundled up, it's time to hit the hills. You might want to start on the small ones first to get the hang of things, but then you can quickly graduate to the bigger hills.

5 Try out different sleds. Everyone seems to have a favorite sled. Some people like to use metal. Others will use plastic. And even others like inflatable tubes. Try them all and see which one you like. Some work better on certain types of snow than others.

Jack's Top Tips and Takeaways

- **Go at night.** Try night sledding for a really cool experience. Of course, not just any hill is good for night sledding. Be sure to go to a place that offers night sledding because they'll have lights.

- **Buy good gloves.** Buy and wear gloves that will be able to hold up against all the snow and water. This way your hands aren't soaked and freezing after just a few runs down the hill.

- **Keep some distance.** If you want to challenge a friend to a sled race down the hill, be sure you're far enough apart. This way, if either sled goes off its path, you won't hit each other.

87
HAVE AN EPIC SNOWBALL FIGHT.

ONE EPIC SNOWBALL FIGHT just isn't enough. You have to have at least one every season. Here are the tips for having a truly amazing, wonderful, and totally epic snowball fight.

1 Invite your most epic friends. A really good snowball fight involves lots of people. You can recruit family members, friends, and neighbors. A good group would be ten or more people. So as soon as you get a good snowfall, put out a notice and get lots of people to participate.

2 Pick teams and set rules. Your rules can be as simple or as complicated as you like. Do you just want it to be a fun experience and there aren't really any rules? Would you like to do a scoring system of some sort every time someone hits a target? You don't have to be formal, but it can be fun to turn it into a game/adventure.

3 Create lots of epic snowballs before the fight begins. You should make twice as many snowballs as you think you'll need because they will go fast. Be sure to pack them well so they stick together. You don't want them to fall apart as soon as you pick them up.

4 Add a little bit of fun to your snowballs. Maybe you have some snowballs with a saying. Or perhaps you dye the snowballs different colors or throw some glitter in the mix. Use your imagination to make the snowballs stand out.

5 Let the epic battle commence. Three . . . two . . . one . . . go! Once everyone has a position and has snowballs, it's time to start throwing. Remember to follow the rules (if you set them), and then celebrate with hot chocolate when you're all done.

Jack's Top Tips and Takeaways

- **Make 'em stick.** You can make snowballs stick together better by adding just a little bit of water. You don't want to add too much because it'll turn them to ice, which can hurt someone when you hit them. (By the way, it's a good idea to make a rule not to throw at anyone's face.) But a spray bottle with just a little bit of spray can help hold the snowballs together.

- **Add a point system.** One way to add a game to your snowball fight is to write down different points on pieces of paper and fold the papers up and put them in the center of the snowballs. People can pick up the pieces of paper, and whatever number is on them counts as points for their team.

- **Combine this one with fort building.** Why not make fort building and a snowball fight a combined activity? These would be awesome to put together. Both teams can build their own fort, and then you can make a bunch of snowballs to have a friendly fight.

88

GO ICE SKATING.

YOU DON'T HAVE TO LIVE IN THE COLD to go ice skating. While it is cool to skate on an actual outdoor rink, there are ice-skating rinks all over the country. Just find one in your area, and give this sport a try for yourself.

1 Find a place to go to that has good rentals. Look up the places to ice skate in your area, and be sure to check their hours. You also want to make sure they have good rental options so you don't have to invest in new skates for a sport you just want to try out. You might even call ahead to see if they have any beginner lessons where you can get an overview from a pro. Sometimes these are offered during busy times as a quick introduction to the sport.

2 Try some basic moves. Most ice-skating instructors will have you start with a march on the ice. This will get you used to the feel of skates on your feet, and it really is like a march. As you get the hang of this, you'll then start setting your foot down and gliding slightly outward. These should be small movements, and as you get more confident you can glide a little more each time.

3 Learn how to stop. Imagine your feet are parallel and together as if you were just skating. As you get ready to stop, both feet go slightly outward. Then one skate should turn sideways to help stop your motion forward.

4 Practice falling. This is actually pretty important to learn if you want to keep from hurting yourself. If you feel yourself start to fall, you should bend your knees slightly and fall forwards and sideways. This will keep you from falling backwards, which could lead to a head injury. By the way, helmets are totally fine to wear on the ice if you're just starting out.

5 Keep practicing and adding on a little at a time. Speed and movement will come with time. You can't expect to be good at ice skating after just one time. Keep practicing or even take lessons, and you'll learn more techniques and skating methods as you go.

Jack's Top Tips and Takeaways

- **Don't look down.** You will probably want to look down, but this isn't always a good idea. In fact, it can actually make you lose your balance more. Try to keep your eyes up.

- **Get a good fit.** If you do decide to invest in skates, go to a skate shop so they fit you properly.

- **Don't use too many layers.** You do want to stay warm, but as you skate around the rink, you'll quickly warm up. So don't have so many layers on that you'll get too sweaty on the ice.

≡ 89 ≡
MAKE A UNIQUE SNOWMAN.

MAKING A SNOWMAN IN WINTER is also something you should do every single year. Well, as long as you have enough snow. But once you've done that a few times, you might be ready to take it to the next level and make a different kind of snowman instead.

1 Research amazing snowmen online. Many people have gotten tired of making the same old snowman, and they've invented their own. Then they take pictures and post them to social media sites like Pinterest and Instagram, so you have somewhere to get inspiration. Look on these sites or even Google images for "unique snowman" and see what you find. For instance, how about a detective, superhero, or minion?

2 Gather the supplies to make a creative snowman. If you're dressing up a snowman in a unique way, you'll need to gather the supplies. For instance, if you're doing a minion, you might need a spray bottle with yellow food coloring to turn the snow yellow. If you're creating a detective, you need the right hat and cape.

3 Construct your snowman. Now put your snowman plan into action. Be sure to build it in a visible area like the front yard so others can appreciate your design. Details matter for snowmen like this, so think about every little eye, button, and accessory.

4 Now try making a snow animal. After you've mastered a snowman, challenge yourself to create a snow animal. For instance, a snow dog, a snow bunny, or a snow elephant would be good creations.

5 Finally, make a unique snow creature. Now it's time to make something totally out of the ordinary. Move away from a snowman or animal, and dream up something completely different. Perhaps it'll be a snow monster, yeti, or alien!

Jack's Top Tips and Takeaways

- **Try one upside-down.** An upside-down snowman is a great and easy way to do a fun snowman. You'll have to make a strong base because it gets larger as you go up, but it's totally possible.

- **Have a neighborhood competition.** Get your neighbors involved. Put out a flyer or challenge a few neighbors to a snowman or snow creature competition. It'll look so cool to have several in a single neighborhood.

- **Look for heavy snow.** This is best for packing in the snow and making your creation strong and secure. You might have to dig a little bit to find good snowman-building snow.

90
HAVE A WINTER BONFIRE.

YOU'LL FIND PLENTY OF BONFIRES in spring, summer, and fall, but what about winter? Most people might not think of having a bonfire in winter, but it's actually a great time. You might have to bundle up a little bit more and throw on some gloves, but it's definitely worth it.

1 Whether you're in the backyard or somewhere else, bonfires are more fun with friends. Set a date, and then invite friends over for a bonfire. Let them know that you will be outside, so they need to dress for the weather. You could also make it a potluck and have everyone bring something to make it a full experience.

2 Carve out a place for your fire. If you already have a fire pit or outdoor fireplace, just uncover it, brush away the snow, and get it ready for your fire. If you don't have a designated spot, you can build one with rocks, bricks, or other material that will help contain the fire. You might not think this is necessary because it's winter (i.e., cold) and you assume the fire won't get out of hand. But it's still really important to take these fire safety precautions.

3 Build up your fire with sticks and logs. Have you already mastered a good fire from the camping chapter? You want to use these same techniques, creating a tepee shape with logs and plenty of airflow beneath the logs. Use small sticks or kindling in between the large logs to help the fire get a good start.

4 Light your fire, and keep it fed. Again, kindling can help get it started, but if that doesn't work, you might try newspaper or fire starter material. As the fire gets going, be sure to feed it with logs. You might use more logs and create a bigger fire than you would in summer because you need the extra warmth. Just be sure to keep an eye on it at all times.

5 Make hot dogs or s'mores, just like you'd do in summer. Once you have a good fire going, bring out the s'mores, hot dogs, or whatever else you love making over the fire. Anything you make in the summer is perfectly fine to make in the winter, too. If you happen to have access to a dutch oven or a big pot, soup is also a really awesome option to make outdoors over the fire.

Jack's Top Tips and Takeaways

- **Make winter fire starters.** You can create a great fire starter using a pinecone. It's similar to the process of making candles. You use a wax mixture and dip the pinecone and add a wick. You can find a video tutorial for this on YouTube.

- **Make a ring.** It helps to have your fire outlined with rocks, bricks, or cement blocks. This helps keep your fire contained, and it helps others to know what area is safe.

- **Designate a fire captain.** For an extra safety measure, have one person be on fire watch at all times, so he can never turn his back on the fire. If he leaves the area, even to go to the bathroom, someone else has to take on this duty.

COOKING

"FIND SOMETHING YOU ARE PASSIONATE ABOUT AND KEEP TREMENDOUSLY INTERESTED IN IT."

—JULIA CHILD

Cooking and baking are great skills to have in general. Once you learn a few basic recipes, you'll be able to make these for many years. And if you throw in an outdoor or nature element into cooking and baking, it makes it even more rewarding.

In this chapter you'll learn how to make several items that make the most of garden favorites like fruits, veggies, and herbs. Have you heard the phrase "farm to table" at all? This is pretty much what you're doing when you use items from local farms and gardens. You're taking food directly from farms and cooking with it. But, first things first. Let's start off with something every outdoorsy person should master—your own trail mix.

91

CREATE YOUR OWN TRAIL MIX.

TRAIL MIX HAS A LONG HISTORY of keeping hikers energized on the trail. There's a reason it's so popular. It's an easy snack to throw in your day pack because it doesn't need a lot of space or to be kept refrigerated. Plus, the fruit and nuts in these mixes can help give you a burst of energy when you need it most.

1 Learn the basics of what's in trail mix. If you look at trail mix recipes or pictures, you'll see that the basics include nuts, like peanuts, almonds, and pecans, as well as dried fruits, like cranberries, cherries, blueberries, raisins, and more. You'll also see lots of recipes with small chocolate pieces, like chocolate chips or M&Ms.

2 Research trail mix recipes you can try. Now that you know the basics, start looking up trail mix recipes online. Really search for unique or unusual recipes to give you ideas of what else can make up trail mix. Marshmallows anyone? How about toffee pieces? This will help give you ideas for creating your own.

3 Now start experimenting. If you can dream it up, you can definitely try it in trail mix. You'll want to stick to dry ingredients to keep the mix mess-free while on the trail. But pretty much anything goes. Some of the ingredients you might want to try include dry cereal, mango, wasabi peas, and chocolate-covered sunflower seeds. You might also experiment with using different herbs or seasonings with your mix to give it extra flavor.

4 Test your recipe out on the trail. You want to make sure you like it and it works. Don't load up your recipe with chocolate because it's not ideal for getting energy on the trail. (Well, you get energy, but then you could have a sugar crash!) You might even try a few different recipes on a long hike or trip so you can figure out your favorite.

5 Now that you've tested them out, it's time to make adjustments. Maybe you love certain fruits and you want to load up on those. Or perhaps you want to do a ranch-flavored mix, using a dry-mix pack. Then, when you have that great recipe, be sure to write it down so you can make it again easily.

Jack's Top Tips and Takeaways

- **Make it sustainable.** Try to avoid using plastic bags to house your mix. Package your trail mix in a biodegradable package that is more environmentally friendly.

- **Freeze it.** If you use chocolate in your mix and it's going to be hot, try freezing it the day before so it'll last on your hike.

- **Get a few taste testers.** As you're experimenting, it's important to have taste testers. Get feedback on what people like, and adjust your recipe accordingly as you go.

92
MAKE YOUR OWN SALSA.

SUMMER IS THE PERFECT TIME for making your own salsa. With so many options for fresh tomatoes, you should have plenty on hand to experiment with different flavors and style. Or, if you're not into tomatoes, there are alternative recipes for you, too.

1 Gather up the basics for a traditional tomato salsa. The three essential ingredients in salsa are tomatoes, onions, and peppers (bell peppers or jalapeños). Other common add-ons include cilantro, fresh-squeezed lime juice, and garlic. Then most recipes will call for salt and pepper to taste, which means you can use as little or as much as you like. Gather these ingredients, dice them all up together, and that's it. You have salsa.

2 Now experiment with different peppers and seasonings. Every salsa recipe can be adjusted as you see fit. If you like spicy peppers, switch out the bell peppers for jalapeños. If you have a seasoning you like to cook with, try adding a little bit of it into your salsa. You can also experiment with how much of each item you use. For instance, some people don't like cilantro, so they'll skip it. Others really like lime, so they'll squeeze lots of limes for the salsa.

3 Tomatoes aren't the only seasonal salsa people like to make. Two other popular options are watermelon salsa and mango salsa. Both recipes are simple, and you can find them online. They're also good to eat with pita chips.

4 Give salsa verde a try. This salsa is made from tomatillos, and it's actually really easy to make. You'll peel the tomatillos from their shell-like outer layer. Then you roast them in the oven for a bit until the tomatillos are lightly browned. Once cool, blend them into salsa and add similar ingredients as you would for the traditional tomato salsa.

5 Invent your own salsa. After you've made some of these basic salsa recipes, try creating your own. Maybe you want to mix ingredients like tomatillos and regular tomatoes or mango and watermelon. Let your imagination dream up something unique and amazing.

Jack's Top Tips and Takeaways

- **Chop, chop.** You can have chunkier salsa or smoother salsa, depending on what you like. If you like it chunkier, chop your ingredients bigger. If you like it smooth, you might use an electric chopper or blender on the ingredients.

- **Make it last.** If you have a lot of tomatoes one year and have a lot of salsa, think about canning the salsa. This way you can eat it later or use it in other dishes.

- **Use the right tomatoes.** The ripeness of the tomato matters. Ripe and juicy red tomatoes will give you better flavor. Try not to use green tomatoes.

= 93 =
LEARN HOW TO MAKE JAM.

IF YOU HAVE FRESH FRUIT ON HAND, you definitely don't want it to go to waste. One great way to use it, especially in summer when it's easy to find, is to make your own jam. More specifically, freezer jam is the easiest way to go.

1 Find a basic freezer jam recipe. Freezer jam is one of the easiest recipes you'll ever make. A lot of people are surprised it's so easy to turn their favorite fruit into jam, but it really only takes three ingredients (or sometimes four). This includes fruit, sugar, pectin, and sometimes lemon juice.

2 Gather up the fruit you want to use, and chop it up. Any berry-based fruit will have similar instructions for freezer jam. Fruits that are good options include blueberries, strawberries, raspberries, and blackberries. You can also try plums, peaches, cherries, and mangoes. You'll want to chop up your fruit pretty well for the best results. Some people like to leave chunks (especially with fruit like strawberries), but the other options tend to do better if the fruit is entirely blended.

3 Heat up the fruit mixture, and add the pectin and sugar. Pectin, usually found in the baking aisle, is the magic ingredient that turns your blended fruit into more of a gel. Nearly all pectin boxes will have freezer jam recipes inside, so consult the directions for this next part to get the right ratios. But basically, you add your other ingredients at this time, and then you heat it all up to help activate the pectin.

4 Once your mixture starts cooling, it's time to put the jam in the jars. (A lot of people will sanitize and preheat the jars, so check the specific directions you're following.) After you fill the jars, place the lids on and then put them in the freezer. If you're planning to use the jam right away, you can place it in the fridge instead. Otherwise, keep it in the freezer until it's time to use it.

5 Mix up your favorite fruits to create a whole new recipe. It's always good to follow a recipe when you first start, but then it's fun to experiment. Try mixing two or three fruits together for a unique flavor.

Jack's Top Tips and Takeaways

- **Mix it together.** One of my favorite ways to do jam is to mix berries together. A good mixture I like is raspberries, blueberries, and blackberries. Another fun combo to try is raspberries and pomegranate.

- **Try a low-sugar option.** Most pectin boxes give you an option to make a low-sugar recipe. Try it. It doesn't actually reduce the flavor that much. You might really like it.

- **Prep your berries correctly.** As you collect and prep your ingredients for your jam, make sure to get rid of any bad spots and stems. You don't want to have a bitter or bad taste in your jam.

94
COOK WITH YOUR GARDEN HERBS.

HERBS ARE POPULAR GARDEN PLANTS because they are so useful, adding flavor and spice to your favorite dishes. Yes, you can use dried herbs that come from a jar, but you just can't beat the taste of fresh ones that come straight from your garden.

1 Use cilantro in your favorite Latin dishes. Not everyone loves cilantro (some people say it tastes soapy), but if you do like it, try using it in enchiladas, tacos, and your fresh salsa. Cilantro can be a little bit challenging to grow, so if you can't get it established, buy it fresh from a farmers' market instead. Another trick is to plant new cilantro every few weeks during spring and summer so you can have a long harvest. Just pick off the leaves of the plants, mince, and throw it in with your other ingredients.

2 Throw chives in with just about anything. This is an easy herb to grow, and it's really easy to cook with. Use it to add flavor and spice in just about any dish. Some people use it like they would onions, but it's also good chopped up in salads, soups, and more.

3 Make pesto with your fresh basil. Basil is a popular herb to grow, and it's great on a fresh caprese (tomato) salad or on a pizza. In addition to being great fresh, it's an herb you can chop up to make something else—pesto. Pesto uses olive oil and pine nuts, along with a lot of fresh basil. Look up a recipe to try, and then make your own. This will be so good on crackers or tossed with noodles.

4 Mint is also easy to grow, and while it smells great, some people struggle with knowing what to do with it. An easy (and yummy) way to use it is to put it in your favorite summer drink. A lemonade, limeade, or just water can gain a unique flavor when you add a few mint leaves. It doesn't take much, so start with a few leaves and then increase the amount you use a little bit at a time.

5 Add thyme and rosemary to your main dishes. Both of these are popular to mix with protein, like chicken, pork, and beef. If you have a favorite dish, experiment with adding thyme and rosemary. Just a little bit will add a lot of flavor.

Jack's Top Tips and Takeaways

- **Eat more cilantro.** This is my favorite herb, and it works with lots of flavors. A lot of people think of cilantro as being best for Latin dishes, but it's also good in a lot of Asian cuisine. Give it a try.

- **Grow herbs year-round.** These are herbs you can grow outside in your garden, but you can also try growing them in winter, too. It's a good challenge to grow herbs indoors, and you'll love cooking with them all year.

- **Experiment on your own.** A lot of people think that some herbs are good in only certain dishes. But the truth is that herbs can be mixed up in all types of cuisines. Test out different herbs and flavors to see what you most like.

95

DRY YOUR OWN FRUITS OR VEGETABLES.

WHEN YOU HAVE FRESH FRUITS AND VEGGIES, you wish you could make them last as long as possible. One way to do this is by drying them for eating in later seasons. There are a few ways to dry your own fruits and veggies, so take your pick.

1 First, learn which fruits and veggies are best for drying. You can try just about anything, but you'll have the best luck with apples, strawberries, peaches, bananas, and apricots. For veggies, try carrots, green beans, or corn.

2 Do the right prep work. If you're drying your fruits or veggies in pieces, you'll want to cut them into slices. You also want to use fruit that is free of brown spots or marks—fresh fruits and veggies that aren't overly ripe will work best.

3 Use a dehydrator for drying. If you've never used a dehydrator before, it's kind of awesome. It should have instructions, or you can look up guidelines online. You can put fruits or veggies in here for a few hours to a few days, and it's almost magical how they turn into dried eats.

4 Another way to make dried fruits or veggies is to just use your oven. Most of the time, you'll put the oven on a very low temperature. Then you'll place your items in the oven for several hours, rotating or flipping occasionally. You can look online for

these guidelines, as well. This is a good way to test out drying fruit or veggies because almost everyone has access to an oven.

5 Try the sun to dry your fruits and veggies. If you want to have the full nature experience, then dry fruits and veggies in the sun. You can make or buy special outdoor drying racks with mesh bottoms. Otherwise, cookie sheets will work, too. You need patience and lots of hot sun to do this method. Keep in mind that you will need to keep the food protected from animals and the weather. It does take more time and work, but there's something really cool about saying the sun did all the work.

Jack's Top Tips and Takeaways

- **Make your own fruit roll-ups.** Fruit leather (which is like fruit roll-ups) is also yummy to make. You can try different recipes. Most will likely call for a few cups of blended fruit along with a little water or lemon. The smooth mixture, which might have the texture of applesauce, can be spread out on parchment paper for the drying process.

- **Try drying herbs, too.** Just like you can dry fruit, you can also dry herbs for later use. Try using a dehydrator to make herbs you can then store and cook with later in the year.

CREATING

"YOU CAN'T USE UP CREATIVITY.
THE MORE YOU USE,
THE MORE YOU HAVE."

—MAYA ANGELOU

You don't have to DIY or love crafts to make great things from and for nature. Whether you're creating memories, making things for wild animals, or just having fun, here are some of the best projects you can do when it comes to creating.

All of these ideas will give you a great excuse to go outside and take an extra-close look at the world around you. Let them inspire you to come up with your own projects, too.

= 96 =
MOLD AN ANIMAL TRACK.

IF YOU FIND AN ANIMAL TRACK in the wild and it's completely intact, consider making a cast out of it. By using a mixture and letting it sit on the track for a bit, you can have a really cool imprint of the animal track to keep for a long time.

1 Find a track you want to mold in the wild. Don't necessarily pick the first track you come across. Try to find one that is unique. Better yet, find one with a strong outline and definition that shows the entire print.

2 Prep your track area. You'll want to clear away any leaves, sticks, or other items from the track. Then take a narrow strip of cardboard, about an inch or two high, and outline the track in a circular shape, standing the cardboard upright. You'll usually want to leave an inch or two on all sides of the track. This is essentially the little mold/frame you'll use for pouring your plaster.

3 Mix up your casting mixture. The most common mixture to use is a material called Plaster of Paris, which you can buy on Amazon or at a local craft store. You can also look for specific products that are advertised as casting material. When you're ready to cast the animal track, follow the directions on the bag. You don't want to mix it together and add water until you're ready to put it on your track because it will dry. So you might want to wait to mix it up until you're outside and have found the perfect track.

4 Pour your mixture into the track and wait. You really don't need a lot of casting mixture to make a good track. Just pour it in for a thin layer of about half an inch. Then follow the instructions on the bag to learn how long you should wait.

5 Once it's completely dry, gently peel away your cast from the ground. When you do, you should see the animal track you found on the dried mold. You'll be able to keep this cast for a long time. Some people like to paint or decorate it, too.

Jack's Top Tips and Takeaways

- **Practice first.** Before you go out in the wild to put this to the test, you can also try practicing on a dog track. These will be a lot easier to find.

- **Go after the rain.** The best time to find a track is after it's been damp. Look in muddy areas. You don't want it to be too muddy. But just as the mud starts to dry or firm up is a good time to try to get a print.

⌇ 97 ⌇
MAKE A BIRDHOUSE.

GIVE A BIRD IN YOUR NEIGHBORHOOD a home by making your own birdhouse. This is a project you can do any time of year. Then you put it up in the spring and wait for a visitor to fly in and make it a home.

1 Learn about which birds will use birdhouses. You might be surprised to learn that most birds don't actually use birdhouses at all. Instead, they'll nest in trees or other places. However, there are birds that do really like them, and it's a good way to attract birds to your backyard. Some of the bird species that will use a birdhouse include wrens, chickadees, bluebirds, some ducks, and purple martins. To get more info on birds that will (or won't) use birdhouses, check out nestwatch.org.

2 Make note of any specific requirements or dimensions. Of the birds that do use houses, the sizing requirements can be really specific. In particular, you want to pay close attention to the size of the entrance hole on birdhouses. Many birdhouses you buy in the store have holes that are too big, and this makes it easy for other animals and critters to gain access. To build a birdhouse for a specific bird, be sure to look for specific instructions. Again, check out nestwatch.org, and you can find this information for all birds.

3 Start building your birdhouse. Anytime you're working on a woodworking project, you want to measure twice and cut once. This basically means you want to be 100 percent sure of your measurements before you start, because then you won't make mistakes and waste wood or have to redo it.

4 Hang your birdhouse in the right spot. Look at specific requirements for birdhouses once again to gain an overall understanding of where to place a birdhouse. In general, birds will be more likely to use them if they're among trees and shrubs instead of just being out in the open. You might want to have the birdhouse in a good location where you can see it, but having it in a place where the birds will actually go will increase the chance that it'll be used.

5 Wait for the birds to come. It's so hard to be patient, but you have to try. You don't want to move your birdhouse all around or get too close to it. This could scare the birds away. Instead, just watch and wait. Sometimes it takes a season or two for birds to discover it and use it, but it's worth the wait. When you do see a bird move in, give it plenty of space.

Jack's Top Tips and Takeaways

- **Leave it natural.** It's best to leave birdhouses natural instead of painting or staining them. You might like a more colorful color or a cool design. But it'll be more attractive to the birds if you leave it natural.

- **You don't need a perch.** A lot of people think you need a perch on a birdhouse, but this is a myth. In fact, it can actually help predators get into the house. So if you have a choice, leave it off.

- **Get it out early.** If you want to attract birds to nest in your yard, be sure to have your birdhouse out early in the season. Don't wait until the middle of spring or summer to get it out there. Birds will often establish nesting territories early, so you want it ready.

98

PAINT A GARDEN PLANTER.

EXPRESS YOURSELF THROUGH PAINT and a planter. This is a project that anyone can do at any age. Plus, there are so many different ways to paint your planter. The options are endless.

1 Find the perfect container. You can't go wrong with terra-cotta. It's easy to paint and has a nice, clean surface. Most terra-cotta pots don't have a sealant on them at all, so you're able to have a blank canvas to create whatever you want. Some pots will already be sealed or have designs on them, so then they wouldn't make the best options for painting.

2 Gather up the right kind of paint. Watercolors aren't going to cut it. You want to find a paint that is specifically good for the outdoors. Ask at your local craft store for an outdoors paint. Tell them what you're doing for the project, and they'll be able to make a good recommendation.

3 Try personalizing it with fingerprints or handprints. Fingerprints and handprints are awesome all by themselves. However, you can also use them to create animals or other artwork. For instance, a footprint could be the body of a butterfly. Several fingerprints in a row might be perfect for turning into a caterpillar. Look up "fingerprint art" or "handprint art" on Pinterest to get some ideas.

4 Create a specific message. If you're looking to do something different but aren't sure what, try focusing on a single message. It can be simple like "GROW," your name, or a quote you like. You could also plan to put this pot somewhere specific, like on the front porch, where you might want your address on the pot. Don't be afraid to just do something general or a simple phrase.

5 Seal your pot, and then fill it with plants. Even if you're using an outdoors paint that should be waterproof, it's a good idea to seal your pot. You can buy a sealant at a craft store or online. This will help keep your artwork fresh longer. Be sure to put good drainage in your pot, and then fill it up with plants.

Jack's Top Tips and Takeaways

- **Have a painting party.** Turn this into a group activity. Have everyone bring a pot and one color of paint so you can share. This will save you from having to buy all the paint on your own, and it's also just a fun thing to do in a group.

- **Keep it simple.** If you're not sure what to paint but you want a simple design, consider doing a pattern. For instance, just raindrops or flower petals can be done all over your pot in a pattern. It's easy, and it'll look cool.

- **Look online for cool ideas.** Last year, we got my grandma a Harry Potter planter. She loved it, and it was so simple. You can definitely do that one yourself. Just look it up online or on Pinterest, and you'll see how to do it.

99

MAKE SUGAR WATER FOR HUMMINGBIRDS.

HAVING A HUMMINGBIRD FLY up to your porch or backyard is one of the most magical bird experiences you can have. They are so tiny and go so quick, but at the same time, they are completely mesmerizing. Increase your chances of having hummingbirds in your yard by learning how to make sugar water.

1 Learn the basic sugar water recipe. This is one you'll want to memorize. Basically, sugar water for hummingbirds is a four-to-one ratio. This means you'll want four parts water to one part sugar. Based on the size of your sugar-water feeder, this will vary. It might mean four cups of water and one cup of sugar. Or, four half cups of water to one half cup of sugar.

2 Mix your sugar and water, and then boil. You never know if there are impurities in water, so the best thing to do is boil it. Plus, this will help the sugar dissolve better. Put it all in a pan and boil it. Then let it cool completely.

3 Fill your feeder. If you can get a sugar-water feeder that has red on it, then this is the best. Hummingbirds are known

to be attracted to red, which is why so many feeders already feature this color. Some people have even been known to add red elements like bows or fake flowers to their feeder to be even more attractive.

4 Wait for the hummingbirds to arrive. You can increase your chances of attracting hummingbirds by hanging up your feeder during spring or fall migration. This will vary in your area, but you can get specific details and tips at hummingbirds.net.

5 Keep your water fresh. The best thing you can do to keep hummingbirds coming back (or attracting them in the first place) is to have fresh water and a clean feeder. Don't let it get messy or old. This is not attractive to hummingbirds at all.

Jack's Top Tips and Takeaways

- **Keep it pure.** You don't need to dye your water red. A lot of people do this, thinking it'll help, but it doesn't matter. Plus, scientists actually recommend you don't add things to the water. Keep it pure—just sugar and water.

- **Double your chances.** Hang your sugar-water feeder near a hanging basket to give you a double chance of attracting hummingbirds. The flowers hanging near the feeder will help get their attention.

⫶ 100 ⫶
MAKE MUD SLIME.

BRING THE MAGIC OF MUD AND SLIME together with this mud slime recipe. It's so much fun to make, and it's a good reason to go out and get your hands dirty. This recipe is from Jack's sister, Annabelle, who perfected it outside on her own. Thanks, Anna!

1 Gather up the ingredients. You'll need about 1 cup of dirt, 1 cup of water, ¾ cup of glue, and 1 cup of liquid starch. You'll also want to get a container that you can mix the slime in—probably not a cereal bowl or something your parents will miss. Get an old plastic container or something that is OK to stay outside instead.

2 Pour your dirt into the bowl. You'll want to remove any big chunks or rocks in the dirt before you start mixing anything else. Then add your water a little at a time, mixing with a spoon to get a good consistency.

3 Now add your glue a little bit at a time. Mix each time. One of the most important things about making slime is for it to always maintain a good consistency. So it's good to go slowly instead of pouring everything in at once.

4 The final step to making mud slime is adding in your liquid starch. This will be the thing that makes it hold together. As you mix in a little at a time, it'll thicken up and get a slime

consistency. After you mix everything in and the consistency is good, put your spoon aside and start kneading the mixture with your hands. Stretch it out and squish it together until it feels like the perfect slime to you.

5 Store your slime in a plastic container with a lid. If it starts to get too dry or sticky, you might want to add a little more water or liquid starch. It's common for slime to dry up a little bit over time, so this should do the trick to fix that.

Jack's Top Tips and Takeaways

- **Give sand a try.** Try sand in slime, too. You can use a similar recipe as the one above, but you'll just switch out the dirt for sand. It has a gritty texture that is really fun to play with.

- **Play with textures.** Everyone likes different textures. Some people like it more muddy or liquidy while others like it thick. Try a variety of dirt or ratios of your ingredients to see the different results.

- **Keep adding.** When you first start to mix your ingredients, it's going to seem really sticky. You might even think you're doing something wrong. But keep mixing, and trust the process. Don't just add more ingredients right away. It will get a lot better.

101

INVENT YOUR OWN OUTDOOR GAME.

IT'S TIME TO PUT YOUR OWN SPIN on a classic game. Or if you're feeling really creative, come up with a whole new one that no one has heard of before. Your imagination is the star in this activity.

1 Start with what you know. What are your favorite games to play? Do you like really busy, active games that keep you moving? Would you rather sit down and focus on a game in one spot? Think about the games you are naturally drawn to, and let this be your guide for creating your own. You'll be more likely to play a style of game you already like, so it's the perfect place to start.

2 Come up with your own variation of the game Tag. This is a good way to start thinking about challenging yourself and coming up with new ways to play a classic game. How can you reinvent the game Tag? Maybe it has a theme like fairies or zombies. Maybe it uses items like mud or flashlights. Try to put your own spin on Tag to stretch your imagination.

3 Now think of a game you love (that isn't Tag), and come up with a twist. Maybe you love hide-n-seek, and you want to come up with a new way to play. Or perhaps you like Tic-Tac-Toe, and you want to use objects from nature to come up with your own way to play. Anything goes. But it's another good way to stretch your imagination.

4 Try thinking of a whole new game. Now that you've come up with different ways to play classic games, try a different approach and invent a whole new out-of-the-box game. It might borrow some elements of other games, but really push yourself to do something new.

5 Play and test out your games as much as possible. It's good to know that your game will actually work. Test it out on your own. Then invite friends over to play with you. You want to practice your game a lot and be willing to adjust it to make it the best game possible.

Jack's Top Tips and Takeaways

- **Find some sticks.** Try making your own game of pick-up-sticks by gathering up sticks you find outside. It's best to find sticks that are around the same length and size. You can paint them in different colors to make them worth different points.

- **Make your own dice.** I once invented a game that used cardboard to make giant dice. I just folded the cardboard into a cube, and then added numbers to it. It was really fun to play with these biodegradable dice.

- **Keep it natural.** It's fun to use items you find in nature, like rocks or sticks, for your game. Think about how you might be able to use items like this for a game you invent on your own.

ABOUT THE AUTHORS

Stacy and Jack Tornio are a mother-son writing team based in Milwaukee, Wisconsin. Jack is in his teens and has been a nature kid his whole life. He also loves sports, animals, and traveling. Jack is a great gardener and grows his own food every year.

Stacy grew up in Oklahoma, where gardening and being outdoors were just part of her upbringing. She's written more than fifteen books related to gardening, nature, and getting families outside. She also loves writing, editing, and producing video—especially for WeAreTeachers.com.

Stacy and Jack love finding nature opportunities wherever they go. Their favorite places to explore are where they have family in "Up North" Wisconsin and the countryside of Oklahoma. They also enjoy exploring national parks, and they plan to hike the Grand Canyon one day.

You can follow Stacy and Jack's adventures on Instagram (TheDestinationNature) and Facebook (Destination Nature). They also have a website, DestinationNature.com. They would love to hear from you, so be sure to tag them on social media to share your favorite nature spots and sightings.